Ethnic Periodicals in Contemporary America

Recent Titles in
Bibliographies and Indexes in Ethnic Studies

Annotated Bibliography of Puerto Rican Bibliographies
Fay Fowlie-Flores, compiler

Racism in the United States: A Comprehensive Classified Bibliography
Meyer Weinberg

Ethnic Periodicals in Contemporary America

An Annotated Guide

Compiled by
Sandra L. Jones Ireland

Bibliographies and Indexes in Ethnic Studies, Number 3

GREENWOOD PRESS
New York • Westport, Connecticut • London

Research for this bibliography was made possible,
in part, by a grant from
The Reader's Digest Foundation

Library of Congress Cataloging-in-Publication Data

Ireland, Sandra L. Jones.
Ethnic periodicals in contemporary America : an annotated guide / compiled by Sandra L. Jones Ireland.
p. cm.—(Bibliographies and indexes in ethnic studies, ISSN 1046-7882 ; no. 3)
Includes bibliographical references
ISBN 0-313-26817-7 (alk. paper)
1. Ethnic press—United States—Bibliography. 2. American newspapers—Foreign language press—Bibliography. 3. American periodicals—Foreign language press—Bibliography. I. Title. II. Series.
Z6953.5.A1I74 1990
[PN4882]
016.071'3'08693—dc20 90-31737

British Library Cataloguing in Publication Data is available.

Library of Congress Catalog Card Number: 90-31737
ISBN: 0-313-26817-7
ISSN: 1046-7882

First published in 1990

Greenwood Press, 88 Post Road West, Westport, CT 06881
An imprint of Greenwood Publishing Group, Inc.

Printed in the United States of America

The paper used in this book complies with the Permanent Paper Standard issued by the National Information Standards Organization (Z39.48-1984).

10 9 8 7 6 5 4 3 2 1

This guide is dedicated to the Publishers, Editors, Writers, Photographers, Contributors, Advertisers and Readers of ethnic-interest newspapers, newsletters, magazines, bulletins and tabloids.

Ethnic-interest publications are a testament of the belief in the freedom of the press and speech, the expression of ideas, the perpetuation of the creative exchange and a reflection of how we were and where we are in the present.

Contents

Preface

This guide to ethnic-interest periodicals published in the United States was conceived and developed when I needed specific information about ethnic-interest publications and could find nothing which answered my questions.

Primarily, I'm indebted to the editors and publishers of ethnic-interest periodicals who responded to the questionnaire. Their responses, and often candid comments to my inquiries, have provided me with information which makes this guide informative and lively reading. Additionally, some editors provided me with copies of their publications which I found most useful and enlightening. The samples gave me an opportunity to see and to rejoice over the periodicals which contribute to the many facets of the multi-ethnic society and culture in the United States.

The encouragement to pursue answers to my questions about ethnic-interest periodicals came from Marcia Prior-Miller through her course, *Contemporary Magazine Publishing*, (JLMC 341), Fall Semester 1986, offered through the Department of Journalism and Mass Communications, Iowa State University, Ames, Iowa. Professor Prior-Miller suggested I do an independent study project and submit a request for research aid from the Reader's Digest Foundation Travel-Research Grant.

This project was monitored by Zora D. Zimmerman and Phillips G. Davies, Department of English at Iowa State University. Professors Zimmerman and Davies evaluated the project and provided me with valuable input regarding the structure and direction of the project through its many phases. The professional input and encouragement given me by Professors Zimmerman and Davies has been a tremendous asset. I appreciated their interest and willingness to review and edit numerous drafts of the various stages of this project.

Additionally, I wish to acknowledge the support and interest in this project by my husband, Dr. William P. Ireland, who introduced me to the use of word processing and data base records. His knowledge of computers helped me compile the vast amount of data into a manageable form. His input was, and continues to be, valuable.

Special thanks go to my parents, Leland and Leora Jones, Garrison, North Dakota, who patiently stuffed envelopes, mailed and forwarded the responses obtained in the second mailing. Their enthusiasm, support and interest helped me over some hurdles in getting this project completed.

Also on my list of thank-yous, is Dr. James Amend, Chairman of Veterinary Anatomy and Physiology, Atlantic Veterinary College, University of Prince Edward Island, Charlottetown, Prince Edward Island for assistance with photocopy and word processing systems.

When it became necessary for me to work with a translation of my original word processing disks, access and learn another word processing system, Glenda Clements, Blair Vessey and Michelle Gauthier, Atlantic Veterinary College, University of Prince Edward Island, saw to it that my mistakes were kept to a minimum and my sense of humor in "high gear."

And lastly, my editor at Greenwood Press, M. Vasan, deserves many thanks for graciously and patiently guiding me through the complex development of the final manuscript form.

Reference Guide to Data Base Terms

Column 1: Data base terms

ETHNIC INTEREST:	Eth.Int.
PUBLICATION NAME:	Pub.
EDITOR'S NAME:	Ed./Eds.
STREET:	St.
CITY:	City
STATE/ZIP CODE:	St./Zip
TELEPHONE:	Phone
PUBLISHER:	Pub.
SUBSCRIPTION:	Sub.
DISTRIBUTION:	Distr.
CIRCULATION:	Cir.
LANGUAGE USED IN TEXT:	Lang.
% NON-ENGLISH USED IN TEXT:	% non-Eng.
FREELANCE ACCEPTED:	Freelance acc.

Column 2: Data base terms

SELF-ADDRESSED STAMPED ENVELOPE:	SASE
MANUSCRIPT LANGUAGE PREFERENCE:	Ms.lang.prefer
QUERY, LETTER/TELEPHONE:	Query,ltr,phone
MANUSCRIPT LENGTH:	Ms.lgth.
PAYMENT:	Pay
PHOTO: CREDITS/PAY	Photos:Cr./pay
FORMAT:	Mag.,tab.,etc.
SIZE:	Size of pub.
PRINT PROCESS:	B/W/C;Blk/wht/clr
PAPER TYPE:	Newsprint,glossy, etc.
AD TYPE:	Display, classified
DEADLINE:	Deadline
NON-ETHNIC GROUP READERS:	Outside readers
KILL FEE:	Special fee:See description

The standard information and format used in the data base for each ethnic-interest periodical is illustrated above. Due to space limitations in the edited and narrative report, the category labels are not included in each report.

The form for abbreviations used is taken from *Webster's Guide to Abbreviations*; Merriman-Webster, Inc.; Springfield, Massachusetts. 1985.

If a standard abbreviation was not listed in the guide, the abbreviation used is a close approximation to the sound of the word.

Ethnic Interest: The editor/publisher of each periodical was asked to define the ethnic interests of the publication and the readership.

Publication Name: Self-explanatory.

Editor's name: The name of the person, or persons, who reviews manuscripts submitted for publication consideration. This person may be involved in one or more of the publishing processes.

Street, city, zip code: The location of the periodical and address used for correspondence.

Telephone number(s): Self-explanatory.

Publisher: The name of the publisher or the organization responsible for publishing the periodical.

Subscription: The cost for getting the periodical automatically. Some periodicals are sent to members as part of a membership fee.Other forms of subscriptions are: Free; Controlled, sent to a specific group of people who fit pre-determined criteria. Most controlled subscription publications are free to recipient. When the information is available, subscription rates for both the U.S. and international subscribers are provided.

Distribution: The distribution or frequency with which the publication is printed and distributed.

Circulation: When the information is available, circulation numbers for both the U.S. and international subscribers are provided.

Language: Although the periodicals in this book are published in the United States, the language used may not be English.

Percentage of non-English: This category provides additional information about language usage in the periodical.

Freelance accepted: Freelance refers to written, photography and art works. This category provides information about the editorial policy concerning freelance work.

Self-addressed, stamped envelope (SASE): Editors often require an SASE with query letters and manuscripts to facilitate communications. An SASE may or may not be needed for return of original materials to the author.

Manuscript language: The manuscript language preferred.

Query: An inquiry, either by letter or phone, made of an editor, through which a contributor can determine if an idea for freelance work will be acceptable to the editor.

Manuscript length: Some publications have policies which dictate the length of manuscripts, and although this question was not included in the questionnaire, when the information was provided, it is included in the data base. If you have questions about manuscript length, ask the editor.

Payment: The policy for payment can range from no payment to payment in copies.

Photo: Acceptance policy for photos, credits and/or payment.

Format: Broadsheet, bulletin, journal, magazine, newspaper, newsletter, pamphlet and tabloids are examples of various formats.

Size: The size of the periodical is additional format information. color print process.

Paper: The kind of paper used, e.g., bond, glossy, newsprint, semi-glossy and so forth.

Ad type: The type of ads, display and/or classified, used.

Print Process: Black/white, full or partial color

Deadline: The time frame needed for advertising placement.

Non-ethnic group readers: A brief description of readers from outside the group who receive the periodical. For example, libraries, government agencies, embassies, other ethnic groups, people interested in other groups or other group issues and so forth may be among the readers outside the ethnic-interest group.

Kill fee: A fee paid when an assigned article has been cancelled or when the editor wishes to use the idea, but prefers to have staff or established writers develop the article for publication.

Check the list of abbreviations for additional abbreviations used in this guide.

Characteristics of Ethnic-Interest Periodicals

For this book, ethnic-interest periodicals are those publications which have certain minimal characteristics in common. However, this list is not comprehensive nor intended to be limiting. Instead, the list is presented as an overview of the criteria used in this project.

1. Published for and about an audience identified as interested in the social, cultural, religious, economic, education, geographic and political information associated with people who align themselves with a specific ethnic group.

2. The spectrum of news and information published is focused to appeal to the specific group for whom the publication is intended, although there may be others from outside the ethnic group who read and possibly contribute to the periodical.

3. The content of the publications may be for the general or the academic audience or a combination of the two areas. No limiting factors were applied in this regard.

4. Other criteria include (a) the identification of the publication as an ethnic periodical, (b) response to the questionnaire, (c) the publication maintains a mailing list with periodic distribution of the periodical to the names on that list.

5. The following areas have no impact on the above criteria: Mailing area range, print processes, costs, size, length of articles, or number of pages.

Representation of Ethnic-Interest Groups

Ethnic Group identification is group-defined

-A-

African
Afro-American
Afro-Hispanic
Alaska Native
American Indian
Anglo-American Basque
Apache
Arab-American
Arab-Muslim
Armenian
Asian-American
Assyrian-American

-B-

Basque
Bengali
Black
Black-American
Black-Hispanic
British
Byelorussian

-C-

Carpatho-Russian
Celtic
Chicano
Chinese
Chinese-American
Choctaw
Croatian-Yugoslavian
Cuban
Cypriot
Czechoslovakian

-D-

Danish

-E-

Estonian
Ethnic Studies

-F-

Filipino
Filipino-American
Finnish
Finn-American
Franco-American

-G-

German
German-Jewish
Greek
Greek-American

-H-

Hispanic
Hispanic-American
Hungarian

-I-

Indian
Irish
Irish-American
Italian
Italian-American

-J-

Japanese
Japanese-American
Jewish

-K-

Korean

-L-

Latin
Latvian
Lithuanian

-M-

Metis
Mexican-American
Mohawk
Muslim

-N-

Native American
Norwegian

-O, P, Q-

Polish
Polish-American
Portuguese
Portuguese-American

-R-

Romanian
Romanian-American
Russian-American

-S-

Scandinavian
Scottish
Scottish-American
Serbian
Sicilian
Slavic
Slavic-Polish
Slovak
Slovenia

-S-

South American
Spanish

-T-

Tibetan

-U-

Ukrainian
Unknown/undefined

-V, W-

Welsh

-Y-

Yiddish
Yugoslavian

-Z-

Zionist

Use of the Guide

The intent of this guide is to provide basic information in locating and identifying ethnic-interest periodicals published in the United States, but the user should be aware of the following:

While every attempt has been made to provide current and correct information in this guide, the information was gathered over the course of 24 months in 1987-88. Since that time, new publications may have come into being, while others may have moved or ceased publication.

The following suggestions for efficient use of this guide are recommended:

1. Send a query letter and a self-addressed, stamped envelope, (SASE) BEFORE sending a manuscript.

2. If in doubt about the SASE return postage, check with postal clerks before you seal your envelope.

3. If you live in a foreign country and want to contribute to a periodical published in the United States, you will need an International Reply Coupon (IRC) for SASE enclosure. An IRC is the ONLY acceptable postage for pre-paid foreign country return mailing.

4. Even though telephone numbers for many of the publication offices are listed, it is preferable to query in writing. Professional judgment regarding the use of telephone queries should prevail.

5. If you have not seen or read the publication to which you wish to contribute, it is a good idea to get a copy of the publication before

submitting manuscripts. You may be able to obtain copies of the periodical from the library, however, in many instances, it will be necessary to request and purchase a copy directly from the periodical's editor.

6. Your manuscript should be presented on good quality, medium weight paper. Do not use erasable paper as it smudges easily. The copy should be clean, error-free and double-spaced. Always keep a copy of your manuscript.

7. Manuscripts should be presented in letter quality print and printed with a good printer/typewriter ribbon.

8. If you send photographs or art work, each item should be identified. Do not write on the back of a photograph as the imprint of the pencil may show through. Some experts recommend the following:
   Type the photo/art work information on a separate piece of paper and affix to the photo with double-sided tape at mid-point on the back of the photo or illustration. The bottom of the paper should then be folded up over the photograph.

9. If you can't identify the people or places in the photograph, you should not send the photo.

10. Do not send your original photographs, negatives or art work, however the copies you send should be of superior quality.

11. Pack photographs and art work between pieces of cardboard.

12. Send your photographs or art work with the proper manuscript.

List of Abbreviations

-A-

acad...academicians
acc...accepted
admn...administration
adv...advertising
aft...after
agcy...agency
alt...alternate
Am.; Amer...American
anthro...anthropologists
Ap...April
appl...applicable
approx...approximate
art...article
asgn...assign
assoc...association

-B-

bef...before
beg...begin
b.; Blk...Black
B.C.; bdcst...broadcast

-C-

cir.;circ...circulation
class...classified
c.;col.;coll...college
clr...color
col...column
contl...controlled
con...content
contr...contributor
corp...corporation
co...county
cr...credits
cult...culture, cultural

-D-

deadline...deadline
distr...distribution

-E-

ea...each
econ...economists

-E-

ecolo...ecologists
edn...edition
ed...editor
ed...education
ednl...educational
ed...educator
emb...embassy
Engl...English
est.;estab...established

-F-

fr...fathers
fl...flat
fgn.;for...foreign
Fr...French

-G-

genealog...genealogists
Ger...German
govt...government
gp.;gps...group(s)

-H-

hist...history

-I-

indic...indicated
ind...individual
inf...information
inst.;instn...institutions
intl...international

-J-

journ...journalists
Jl...July
Je...June

-K-

-L-

ldr.;ldrs...leader(s)
lgth...length
ltr...letter
lib...library
libs...libraries
ling(s)...linguist, linguists

-M-

ms.;mss...manuscript(s)
M...May
mo...month
mus...museum(s)

-N-

NA...not applicable
N.A...North American
nat...native
natl...national
nec...necessary
newsstd...newsstand
neg...negotiated
N.; Nov...November

-O-

occas...occasionally
org.; orgs...organization(s)
opt...option(s)

-P-

pp...pages
pap...paper
phot...photo, photograph
Pol...Polish
pol.sci...political science
pol...politician
poss...possible
prefer...preference
prefer...preferred
pr...prior
proc...process
prof...professor
pub.; publ...public
pub.; publ...publisher

-Q-

-R-

rdr.;rdrs...reader(s)
req...required
R.;resp...response
res...research
rom...romance
rts...rights
Russ...Russian

-S-

SASE...Self-addressed, stamped envelope
S.; Sept.;Sept...September
svc...service
socio...sociologists
stud...studies
sub(s)...subscription(s)

-T-

-U-

univ...university
unk...unknown

-V-

-W-

wk...week
wht...white
w...wide
wd.;wds...words

-X-

-Y-

yr...year

-Z-

Zion...Zionist

Introduction

The ethnic-interest periodicals in the United States are a reflection of many aspects of our multi-cultural society, and as a source guide to those periodicals, this book provides information on the structure and description of the contents of 290 ethnic periodicals, of which 32 (11%) have multiple ethnic group interests. It is through this information about ethnic-interest periodicals that we can begin to see the rich diversity in our society.

ETHNIC-INTEREST IDENTIFICATION

The definition and/or description of the ethnic interests of the periodicals in this book are defined and described by the editor or publisher of the periodicals. To obtain this information, the questionnaire sent to the editor or publisher of the periodical, a copy of which is included in this book, contained specific questions about the ethnic interests of the periodical. The ethnic group description and definitions were not decided by outside individuals, committees, agencies or criteria.

This inquiry resulted in the identification of 86 ethnic-interest categories, but readers should be aware that this list is far from complete. If a questionnaire was returned with the question on ethnic interests unanswered, this category was listed as unknown. When more than one ethnic group is represented in the periodical, a cross-reference for the other group is given.

In keeping with the emphasis on ethnic group identification, the periodicals are arranged according to the ethnic group to make it easier to find a specific periodical or set of periodicals when only the ethnic group is known.

The index provides more specific information related to the content of the periodicals.

ETHNIC GROUP DEFINITIONS

The self-identification of the ethnic interests of the groups has resulted in the need for the clarification of some of the terms which may seem different or misleading from popular knowledge or understanding.

American Indian: The aboriginal people of North America, South America, and the West Indies, not including the Eskimo groups.
Chicano: People of Mexican-American descent.
Hispanic: American people of Spanish or Latin-American descent.
Indian: People who are natives or inhabitants of India or the East Indies. The secondary definition refers to the Native Americans/American Indians, but for purposes of this book this definition does not apply.
Latin-American: Those countries of the Western hemisphere south of the United States where Spanish, Portuguese or French are official languages. This term also refers to the people who live in these countries.
Latino: People who are natives or inhabitants of Latin America.
Metis: People of mixed American Indian or Native American and French-Canadian ancestry.
Native American: One of the terms used to define the aboriginal people of North America, South America and the West Indies, not including Eskimo groups. The use of this term varies with the tribe and region. Some groups prefer the term American Indian as a distinction from the Eskimo people. Native American may also refer to Hawaiian Polynesian descent.

These definitions were taken from *The American Heritage Dictionary. Second College Edition. Houghton Mifflin Company. Boston. 1982.*

ETHNIC GROUPS AND GEOGRAPHIC AFFILIATIONS

Geographic cross-references are not included in this book as the questionnaire did not contain any questions about the ethnic group's geographical origins or links.

While it may appear that inclusion of geographical information can be easily accomplished, ethnic identity does not equal geographical affiliations or links because through time, various ethnic groups have been displaced, borders have changed and/or political alliances may have influenced the group's geographical affiliations. The inclusion of such information without verification from the group would compromise the ethnic identification research design.

METHODOLOGY

The questionnaire format for this research was developed and reviewed in collaboration with Iowa State University Professors Zora D. Zimmerman and Phillips G. Davies, who were project advisors. The questions were tested for understandability, and the questionnaire design and format were evaluated for ease in answering.

Two mailings were sent. The first mailing was sent to 440 known ethnic periodicals published in the United States, of which 161 (36.5%) responded. The second mailing was sent to the 268 editors and publishers who did not respond to the first mailing, plus six new publications, or 274 questionnaires sent in the second mailing.

There were 73 (26.6%) responses to the second mailing of the questionnaire. This response results in a grand total of 234 (52.4%) responses from a universe of 446 periodicals queried. A third mailing was considered, however, with the decrease in response rate from 36.5 percent in the first mailing to 26.6 percent in the second mailing and no additional research funds, a third mailing was vetoed.

DISCUSSION

During the course of this research, I struggled to find solid basic information such as names, addresses and phone numbers. I found good basic information in *Ulrich's International Directory of Periodicals*, from which I was able to begin direct inquiries. Some of the responding editors and publishers sent me additional names and addresses of other ethnic-interest periodicals not listed. Other sources of information surfaced through reading ethnic-interest periodicals, other journalism-oriented publications, and from friends who are interested in ethnic issues.

The periodicals in this book represent a variety of formats, such as magazines, newspapers, newsletters, tabloids, and bulletins. The printing processes range from black and white photocopies to full color presentation and from newsprint to glossy paper. Regardless of the format, content or the presentation of the publication, these periodicals make it possible for us to see and to better understand those things and ideas shared among people, as well as different group interests and expressions.

Where does the specific information about 30 different publication areas, a description of the editorial content and working information about these publications lead us?

The question is one for the active researcher who wants to investigate and analyze the mass communications of ethnic publications. Ethnic-interest periodicals contain numerous sources of information about audience, content analysis, advertising, language, linguistics, history, immigration and migration patterns, anthropology, sociology and so forth.

Research ideas are only as limited as the researcher's scope of interest and creative thinking processes. These periodicals also provide numerous outlets for freelance writers, photographers and artists.

Comparative data from *Ulrich's International Periodicals Directory* indicates that from 1987 to 1989, the number of ethnic-interest periodicals in the U.S. has increased by 165 new listings. On a world-wide basis, 227 new periodicals have been added to the list. The reasons for the increase in numbers would require more in-depth analysis, but the change in numbers is noteworthy. Presently, this research indicates that most of the information about the ethnic periodicals is a listing of names and addresses with minimal information about the structure and no information about the content of the publication.

These periodicals reflect us as a people descended from different ethnic groups and describe us and our interests today. Very often, the definition of an ethnic group is referred to as other people, yet through this research, it is obvious that everyone is a member of an ethnic group, whether the ethnic group is the majority or the minority group. Perhaps ethnic-interest periodicals speak more about who we are than the well-known daily newspapers and other forms of mass communications.

In closing, the author invites information about ethnic-interest periodicals not listed in this guide.

A

African, Afro-American
AFRICAN STUDIES CENTER NEWSLETTER
Editor: Elizabeth Johnston
100 International Center
Michigan State University
East Lansing, Michigan 48824
(517) 353-1700
Pub.: ASC Michigan State University
Established 1966
Subscription: Free
Distribution: Biannual
Circulation: No data
English text
0% non-English
No freelance articles accepted

SASE: No response
English ms.preference
Query: No response
Ms.lgth.: Not indic.
Payment: No response
Photos: No response
Format: Not indicated
Size: 8.5" x 11"
Black/white
Regular paper
Buff color paper
No advertising
Deadline: Not listed
No outside gp.readers
"Kill" fee: No response

African Studies Center Newsletter is described as containing news about African and some Afro-American events, specifically on topics relevant to the African Studies Center at Michigan State University and graduates of MSU, many of whom are Africans.

This publication does not publish external materials.

(Cross-referenced: Afro-American.)

African, Black-American
BLACK AMERICAN LITERATURE FORUM
Editors: Joe Weixlmann, Carole Gustafson
Indiana State University
Parsons Hall
Terre Haute, Indiana 47809
(812) 237-3169
Publisher: Indiana State University
Established 1967
Sub: U.S.:$15/21; Intl.:$18/21(ind/inst)
Distribution: Quarterly
Cir.: U.S.:1,045; Intl.:69 (Contl./sub.)
English text
0% non-English
Freelance articles accepted

SASE: Required
No ms.language preferred
Query,letter,SASE
No manuscript lgth.given
Pay: Copies
Photos/credits/no pay
Magazine
Size: 6" x 9"
Black/white print
Regular paper
Buff-colored paper
No ads; considering
Deadline: Unknown
Some colleges subscribe
No "kill" fee

The *Black American Literature Forum* is described as a publisher of "belletristic" writing, that is, literature which addresses the aesthetic rather than offering didactic or informative content. The editors indicate an occasional interest in Black American art, film, music and the writing of non-American Blacks.

This publication publishes essays on Black American literature, art and culture, bibliographies, interviews, poems and book reviews. Articles are selected for publication by a twenty-member editorial board of nationally recognized experts in the field of Black American literature and culture.

The editors provided no tips for contributors, but the description of the periodical indicates the focus of the publication. Prospective contributors would probably benefit from obtaining a copy of the periodical before submitting manuscripts for review.

Manuscript evaluation by the editorial board indicates that manuscripts are thoroughly reviewed for content, subject treatment by the author, as well as style.

Authors are provided with eleven copies of the published article as a form of payment.

(Cross-referenced: Black-American.)

African, N.E.African Studies
NORTHEAST AFRICAN STUDIES
Editor: Harold Marcus
African Studies Center
Michigan State University
East Lansing, Michigan 48824
(517) 353-1700
Pub.: African Studies Center; MSU
Established 1979
Sub.: U.S.:$18; Intl.:$18; Africa:$14
Distribution: Quarterly
Circulation: U.S.:400; Intl.:110
French, English text
5-l0% non-English
Freelance articles accepted

SASE: No response
English, French ms.
Query: Not applicable
No ms.lgth.indicated
Payment: Not applicable
Photos: Not applicable
Journal
Size: Not listed
Black/white
Newsprint paper
White color paper
Ads accepted
Deadline: Not listed
Outside group readers
"Kill" fee: Not applicable

Northeast African Studies is a scholarly journal. According to the editor, the journal has a scholarly content which focuses on African Studies and Northeast African Studies.

Freelance articles are accepted, but contributors should be aware of the scholarly intent of this periodical. Contributors would benefit by reviewing a copy of this journal before submitting articles for consideration.

African-American
VIBRATION
Editor: Don Freeman
P.O. Box 08152
Cleveland
Ohio 44108
(216) 432-2790
Publishers: Don and Norma Freeman
Established March 28, 1968
Subscription: U.S.:$4; Intl.:$10
Distribution: Semi-annual
Circulation: U.S.:975; Intl.:25
English text
0% non-English
Freelance articles accepted

SASE: Not applicable
English ms.preference
Query: Not applicable
No ms.lgth.indicated
No payment
Photos/credits/no pay
Magazine
Size: 11" x 12"
Black/white
Glossy paper
White color paper
Ads.: Not indicated
Deadline: Not listed
Libs.,individuals
No "kill" fee

Vibration is published and edited by African-Americans, but the editors say, "(the) mission and message are universal. The periodical is dedicated to the enlightenment of humanity, and according to the editors, thereby contributes to the mental and spiritual empowerment of oppressed peoples and thus their ultimate, total liberation."

With respect to the editorial content of the magazine, the editors write, "The world view expressed in *Vibration* is spiritual in essence and radically humanistic, but not Marxist in its philosophy and thrust. However, it is anti-imperialistic and critical of Western civilization, as well as capitalism, especially the materialistic, hedonistic and egocentric "bottom line" of the West's dominant socio-cultural values."

For contributors, the editors write, "*Vibration* cannot afford to provide financial compensation to contributors, but it can provide new exposure for the writer's or poet's work. However, we do not guarantee that every article or poem submitted will be published.

Afro-American	SASE: Required
AFRICAN AM.FAM.HIST.ASSOC.NEWSLETTER	English ms.preferred
Editor: Herman Mason, Jr.	Query, letter
P.O. Box 115268	No ms.lgth.indicated
Atlanta	No payment
Georgia 30310	Photos/credits/no pay
(404) 755-6391	Magazine
Publisher: Afro.Am.Fam.History Assoc.	Size: 8.5" x 11"
Established 1976	Black/white
Subscription: U.S.:$12 Membership	Other (Bond paper)
Distribution: Quarterly	White color paper
Circulation: U.S.:150; Intl.:0	No ads
English text	Deadline: Not listed
0% non-English	Libs., genealogists
Freelance articles accepted	No "kill" fee

African American Family History Association Newsletter focuses on genealogy and family history, with special emphasis on Afro-American history, genealogy and family history.

The editor provided no tips for contributors.

Afro-American
AFRO-AMERICANS IN N.Y.LIFE AND HISTORY
Editor: Monroe Fordham
P.O. Box 1663
Buffalo
New York 14216
No phone listing
Pub.:Afro-Am.Hist.Assoc.Niagara Frontier
Established 1977
Subscription: U.S:$8; Intl.:$11
Distribution: Biennial
Circulation: U.S.:500 plus
English text
0% non-English
Freelance articles accepted

SASE: No reply
Eng.lang.ms.prefer
Query unnecessary
No ms.length given
No payment
No photos accepted
Format: Not given
Size: 6" x 9"
Black/white
Paper: Not listed
White paper
Display ads
Deadline: Unknown
Interested people
No "kill" fee

The editor of *Afro-Americans in New York Life and History* describes the interests of the periodical's readers in a manner congruent with the title of the publication.

English is the main language used in the periodical, and non-ethnic interest readers are described as "anyone interested in the life and history of Afro-Americans in New York state."

While the editor does not give any specific tips to contributors, freelance articles are accepted. As with any periodical under consideration by a writer, a review of the publication would be helpful before articles are submitted for the editor's consideration.

Afro-American
AMERICAN VISIONS
Editor: Gary A. Puckrein
318 A Street N.W.
Washington
D.C. 20002
(202) 287-3360
Publisher: Visions Foundation
Established January 1986
Subscription: U.S.:$18; Intl.:$30
Distribution: Bimonthly
Circulation: U.S.:30,000
English text
0% non-English
Freelance articles accepted

SASE: Required
English ms.preference
Query, letter
No ms.length indicated
Pay per page
Photos/credits/ASMP rates
Magazine
Size: 8.25" x 11"
Black/white/color
Paper type: Semi-gloss
White color paper
Display, classified
Deadline: Not listed
Outside group readers
"Kill" fee: Per magazine page

American Visions, a bimonthly magazine, publishes articles designed to increase the understanding of the Afro-American culture in history, heritage, fine arts and education.

The editor did not provide any specific tips for contributors.

Afro-American
BLACK WRITER, THE
Editor: Mable Terrell
6919 No. Hale
Chicago
Illinois 60628
(312) 995-5195
Publisher: Terrell Associates
Established 1980
Subscription: U.S.:$18; Intl.:$21
Distribution: Quarterly
Circulation: U.S.: 460; Intl.:40
English text
0% non-English
Freelance articles accepted

SASE: Required
English ms.preferred
Query unnecessary
No ms.length indicated
No payment
Photos/credits only
Magazine
Size: Not listed
Black/white
Glossy paper
White color paper
Display ads
Deadline: 6 weeks before pub.
Colleges receive
No "kill" fee

The Black Writer publishes poetry, articles, fiction and contemporary information articles written by African-American writers in their search for publishers. This periodical reviews progress of African-American writers, and, although *The Black Writer* accepts articles from members only, there is an exception to this rule for scholarly efforts from well-known writers.

The magazine is free to members of International Black Writers Conference(IBWC). The Conference also publishes a newsletter, *In Touch*, and informs its members of various conference workshops, events and competitions such as the McDonald's Literary Achievement Awards for writing about the Black Experience in America and the AMY Writing Awards sponsored by the AMY Foundation. The AMY Foundation is a non-profit corporation which promotes Bible education and invites writers to communicate biblical truth to a secular audience.

The membership fee is structured differently than the subscription fee. Membership is divided into two categories: College students and Senior Citizens pay $8 fee and other members pay $15 fee for annual membership.

The IBWC has local chapters, and members are invited to fill out a writer's profile.

Afro-American
NEW JERSEY AFRO-AMERICAN
Editor: R. Queen
Old address:
460 Central Ave.
East Orange, New Jersey 07018

The survey questionnaire was returned with the notation: "Non-deliverable."

Afro-American
PLAYERS MAGAZINE
Editor: H.L. Sorrell
8060 Melrose Ave.
Los Angeles
California 90046
(213) 653-8060
Publisher: Players International
Established June 1973
Subscription: Subscription/Controlled
Distribution: Monthly
Circulation: U.S.:200,000
English text
0% non-English
Freelance articles accepted

SASE: Required
English ms.preference
Query unnecessary
No ms.length indicated
Pay for freelance
Photos/credits
Magazine
Size: Not listed
Black/white/color
Glossy paper
White color paper
Display ads
Deadline: Not listed
Outside group readers
No "kill" fee

Players Magazine is focused for the African-American reader, and according to the editor, it publishes articles which cover a wide spectrum of interests aimed at young Black men, ages 18-34.

With respect to tips for contributors, the editor writes, "Be contemporary unless dealing with a topic of historical importance."

Afro-American, African
AFRICAN STUDIES CENTER NEWSLETTER
Editor: Elizabeth Johnston
100 International Center
Michigan State University
East Lansing, Michigan 48824
(517) 353-1700
Pub.: ASC Michigan State University
Established 1966
Subscription: Free
Distribution: Biannual
Circulation: No information
English text
0% non-English
No freelance articles accepted

SASE: No response
English ms.preference
Query: No response
No ms.length indicated
Payment: No response
Photos: No response
Format: Not indicated
Size: 8.5" x 11"
Black/white
Regular paper
Buff color paper
No advertising
Deadline: Not listed
No outside gp.readers
"Kill" fee: No response

African Studies Center Newsletter is described as containing news about African and some Afro-American events, specifically on topics relevant to the ASC at Michigan State University and graduates of MSU, many of whom are Africans.

This publication does not publish external materials.

(Cross-referenced: African.)

Afro-Hispanic
AFRO-HISPANIC REVIEW
Editors: Edward Mullen, Marvin Lewis
27 Arts and Sciences Bldg.
University of Missouri
Columbia, Missouri 65211
(314) 882-2030
Pub.: U.Missouri;Black Studies/Rom.Lang.
Established 1982
Subscription: No information
Distribution: 3 per year
Circulation: U.S.:450; Intl.:50
Spanish, English text
50% non-English
No freelance articles accepted

SASE: No response
English ms.preferred
Query: No preference
No ms.length indicated
No payment
No photos
Magazine
Size: Not listed
Black/white
Paper: No response
Paper color: Unknown
No advertising
Deadline: Unknown
Outside group readers
No "kill" fee

Afro-Hispanic Review describes its readership as "those who are interested in the Spanish-speaking Black diaspora."

This periodical is a bilingual journal of Afro-Hispanic literature and culture. It is published jointly by the Department of Romance Languages and the Black Studies Program of the University of Missouri-Columbia.

The *Afro-Hispanic Review* contains literary criticism, book reviews, translations, creative writing and relevant developments in this field of study.

The editors suggest that contributors follow the style recommendations in the *MLA Handbook (1984)*

Alaska Native, Native Amer., Amer.Indian	SASE: Not required
NATIVE PRESS RESEARCH JOURNAL	English ms.prefer
Eds.: D.F.Littlefield, J.W.Parins	Query unnecessary
502 Stabler Hall	No ms.length indic.
University of Arkansas	No payment
Little Rock, Arkansas 72204	No photos
(501) 569-3160	Magazine
Pub.: American Native Press Archives	Size: Not listed
Established Spring 1986	Black/white
Sub.: U.S.:$12; Intl.:$12; Inst./Free to Native Am.	Heavy bond paper
Distribution: Quarterly	White color paper
Circulation: U.S.:745; Intl.:5	No ads
English text	Deadline: Unknown
0% non-English	Acad.,St.Pub.libs.
Freelance articles accepted	No "kill" fee

Native Press Research Journal publishes scholarly articles on American Native publishing, journalism, journalists, etc., as well as profiles of current or historical American Indian and Alaska Native periodicals.

This periodical is free to Native American and Alaska Native tribal groups. Outside groups which subscribe and receive the journal are academic, state and public libraries.

The editors say that no editorials are published and that views expressed in the academic articles do not necessarily reflect the views of the editors.

The editors further write that the publisher of the journal is a "poor" academic department; thus no payments can be given to contributors whose articles are published.

With respect to suggestions for prospective contributors, the editors write, "Get a copy of the first issue and see what our publishing goals are; then look at subsequent issues to see the kinds of topics we publish.

"Success depends on aiming at our audience as it does in any kind of writing. We seek well-researched articles or authoritatively-written articles by those who have been involved in the native press."

(Cross-referenced: Alaska Native, American Indian and Native American.)

American Indian
AMERICAN INDIAN LAW NEWSLETTER
Editor: Marc Mannes
P.O.Box 4456; Station A
Albuquerque
New Mexico 87196
(505) 277-5462
Pub.: American Indian Law Center, Inc.
Established 1968
Sub.: U.S.(Am.Ind.);$15; (Gen.pub.) $20
Distribution: Bimonthly
Circulation: U.S.:600; Intl.:100
English text
0% non-English
Freelance articles accepted

SASE: Required
English ms.preferred
Query, letter
No ms.length indicated
No payment
No photos
Magazine
Size: 8.5" x 11"
Black/white
Regular paper
Cream color paper
Ads: No information
Deadline: Unknown
Libs.,Govt.,others
No "kill" fee

American Indian Law Newsletter publishes articles concerning American Indian Law and related subjects.

With respect to tips for contributors the editor writes, "We use only articles dealing with current issues or topics concerning American Indian Law." The editors do not use freelance ideas.

American Indian
EAGLE'S EYE
Editor: Ken Sekaquaptewa
B.Y.University Multicultural Programs
240 KMB
Provo, Utah 84602
(801) 378-6263
Publisher: BYU Multicultural Programs
Established 1965
Subscription: U.S.:$10; Intl.:$15
Distribution: Three/academic year
Circulation: No response
English text
0% non-English
Freelance articles accepted

SASE: Required
No ms.lang. preferred
Query, letter
No ms.length indicated
No payment
Photos/credits/no pay
Magazine
Size: 9" x 12"
Black/white/color
Glossy paper
White color paper
No advertising
Deadline: Not listed
Libs.,museums,schools
No "kill" fee

Eagle's Eye, a publication of Brigham Young University's Multicultural Programs, is described as being written for the University's American Indian students.

The editor did not provide any special tips for contributors.

American Indian
EAGLE, THE
Editor: Jim Roaix
P.O. Box 579 MO
Naugatuck
Connecticut 06770
(203) 274-7853
Publisher: Eagle Wing Press, Inc.
Established November 1981
Subscription: U.S.:$10-15; Intl.:$15-25
Distribution: Bimonthly
Circulation: U.S.:1,100; Intl.: 24
American English text
1% (less than) non-English
Freelance articles accepted

SASE: Required
English ms.preferred
Query unnecessary
No manuscript length indicated
No payment
Photos/credits/no pay
Tabloid
Size: 11" x 17"
Black/white
Newsprint paper
White color paper
Display
Deadline: 2 weeks before pub.
Schools, libraries subscribe
No "kill" fee

The Eagle is described as having American Indian interests. The editor says, "The less than one percent non-English words or phrases are from the various native languages."

This publication is further described as a "positive press as much as possible, but is trying to expose practices that are stereotypical."

The editor's tips to contributors: "We are an all-volunteer group. We pay only in copies of issues. We are looking for historical pieces on American Indians, crafts, literature, news items, features, and prefer pieces written by American Indians, but well-written, knowledgeable writings by others do appear, and we can use them."

American Indian
EARLY AMERICAN
Editor
General Delivery
Fredonia, Arizona 86022-9999

The questionnaire was unclaimed and no forwarding address provided.

American Indian
INDIAN CRUSADER
Editor: Basil M. Gaynor
4009 S.Halldale Ave.
Los Angeles
California 90062-1851
(213) 299-1810
Pub.: Am.Indian Liber.Crusade, Inc.
Established 1952
Subscription: U.S.: Donation
Distribution: Quarterly
Circulation: U.S.: 4,026; Intl.: 6
English text
0% non-English
No freelance articles accepted

SASE: Not applicable
English ms.preferred
Query: No response
No ms.length indicated
No payment
No photos accepted
Newspaper
Size: 8.5" x 11"
Black/white
Glossy paper
White color paper
Ads: No information
Deadline: Not listed
Radio B.C.listeners
"Kill" fee: Unknown

Indian Crusader publishes articles about American Indians, but the editor writes that the readers are nearly all "Anglo."

Many of the subscribers are people who listen to the radio broadcasts, and in turn, the listeners send in a donation and a request to be put on the mailing lists.

The editor writes, "We try to portray the condition of the Indians on the reservations of the United States, particularly in the Southwest and in North Carolina."

There were no tips for contributors.

American Indian, Alaska Native, Nat.Amer.
NATIVE PRESS RESEARCH JOURNAL
Eds.: Daniel F.Littlefield, J.W. Parins
502 Stabler Hall
University of Arkansas
Little Rock, Arkansas 72204
(501) 569-3160
Publisher: Amer.Native Press Archives
Established Spring 1986
Sub: U.S.:$12; Intl.:$12; Free: Native Americans
Distribution: Quarterly
Circulation: U.S.:745; Intl.: 5
English text
0% non-English
Freelance articles accepted

SASE: Unnecessary
English ms.prefer
Query unnecessary
No ms.lgth.indic.
No payment
No photos
Magazine
Size: Not listed
Black/white
Heavy bond paper
White color paper
No ads
Deadline: Unknown
Libraries
No "kill" fee

Native Press Research Journal publishes scholarly articles on

American Native publishing, journalism, journalists, etc., as well as profiles of current or historical American Indian and Alaska Native periodicals.

The *Native Press Research Journal* is free to Native American and Alaska Native tribal groups. Outside groups which subscribe and receive the journal are academic, state and public libraries.

The editors say that no editorials are published and that views expressed in the academic articles do not necessarily reflect the views of the editors.

The editors further write that the publisher of the journal is a "poor" academic department, thus no payments can be given to contributors whose articles are published.

With respect to suggestions for prospective contributors, the editors write, "Get copy of the first issue and see what our publishing goals are; then look at subsequent issues to see the kinds of topics we publish.

"Success depends on aiming at our audience as it does in any kind of writing. We see well-researched articles or authoritatively-written articles by those who have been involved in the native press."

(Cross-referenced: Alaska Native, American Indian and Native American.)

American Indian, Metis
PAN-AMERICAN INDIAN ASSOC.NEWS
Editor: Chief Piercing Eyes
P.O. Box 244
Nocatee
Florida 33864
(813) 494-6930
Publisher: Chief Piercing Eyes
Established January 1984
Subscription: U.S.:$12; Intl.:N/A
Distribution: Three to five/year
Circulation: U.S.:4,500; Intl.:50
English text
0-1% non-English
Freelance articles accepted

SASE: Not required
English ms.preferred
Query unnecessary
Ms.length.: 1 -2 pages
No payment
Photos/credits/no pay
Tabloid
Size: Not listed
Black/white
Newsprint paper
White color paper
Display ads
Deadline: Not listed
Anthro.,ecolog.,New Age
No "kill" fee

Pan-American Indian Association News, formerly *The Tribal Advisor*, is described by the editor as "seeking to help Indian and Metis recapture or discover their ancient heritage and apply it to a modern world, with a heavy emphasis on genealogy and its genetic and spiritual implications and revival groups, including how to start a revival group and so forth."

The editor, Chief Piercing Eyes, in describing the editorial content of the periodical, writes, "(Publication) of a practical understanding of issues pertaining to the reviving Indian. We seek to correct misunderstanding of traditionalism, especially in revival groups. While the whole matter of genetic upsurge and returning to traditional values is taken in deadly seriousness, it is pursued in a lightly humorous vein without too much doomsday.

"If it isn't fun, it probably isn't worth doing.

"We try to avoid revenge and violence and emphasize 'getting even' through exposure and good humor. We don't want outsiders afraid of us or other revival groups," Chief Piercing Eyes writes of the publication.

For contributors, the editor comments, "Camera-ready copy in 5" columns ready to clip and paste greatly tempt us to use them. Send for a free sample copy to study. Nothing illegal. Violence only in historical sense. We want materials that emphasize displaced Reservation Indians 'getting along' in modern society without losing traditional identity (a tricky exercise), and we want revival Indians to gain a sense of destiny and avoid revenge fantasies. Don't take yourself too seriously. Let's enjoy reviving our heritage."

(Cross-referenced: Metis.)

American Indian, Native American	SASE: Not indicated
AMER.INDIAN CULTURE AND RESEARCH JOUR.	English ms.preferred
Editor: Hanay Geigomah	Query unnec.;ltr.o.k.
3220 Campbell Hall	No ms.lgth.indicated
University of California-Los Angeles	No pay for articles
Los Angeles, California 90024-1548	No photos/cr./no pay
(213) 825-4777	Magazine
Pub.: American Indian Studies Center	Size: 130 page lgth.
Established 1976	Black/white
Sub.: U.S.:$20/yr.; Intl.:$21/yr.	Glossy paper
Distribution: Quarterly	White color paper
Circulation: U.S.:650; Intl.:50	Display
English text	Deadline: Not listed
0% non-English	Profs.: hist., myth.
Freelance articles accepted	No "kill" fee

American Indian Culture and Research Journal is written for people interested in any significant research or topic about Native Americans and/or for those who have concerns regarding American Indians.

Outside group readers include anthropologists, English or literature professors, policy-makers and lawyers in addition to the above listing.

Papers submitted to the journal are "blind-refereed papers by three or more referees. The editors invite comments on scholarly and policy issues, but the editorial staff does not write editorials."

The editors suggest contributors follow the guidelines in the journal for submission of articles.

(Cross reference: Native American.)

American Indian, Native American	SASE: Required
WHISPERING WIND MAGAZINE	English ms.preference
Editor: Jack B. Heriard	Query unnecessary
8009 Wales Street	No ms.length indicated
New Orleans	Pay in copies only
Louisiana 70126-1952	Photos accepted
(504) 241-5866	Magazine
Pub.: Louisiana Indian Herit.Assoc., Inc.	Size: 8.5" x 11"
Established October 1967	Black/white
Sub.: U.S.: $12; Int.:$14	Glossy paper
Distribution: Bimonthly	White color paper
Cir.: U.S.:3,875; Intl.:125	Display, classified
English text	Deadline: 60 da.before pub.
05 non-English	Lib.,prisons,N.A.enthusiasts
Freelance articles accepted	No "kill" fee

According to the editor of *Whispering Wind Magazine*, 59 percent of the readers are American Indian. Among the non-ethnic interest readers, the editor lists libraries, prisons, youth groups, American Indian enthusiasts who have a sincere interest in the American Indian, but who are not American Indian, as magazine subscribers.

The magazine contains articles about American Indian crafts and material culture, past and present. Historical manuscripts relating to the American Indian are published and the magazine is fully illustrated.

The editor's tips for contributors are as follows:

"Articles should be submitted typed, double-spaced and in duplicate. One set of photos, if necessary for the article, should accompany the manuscript.

"Illustrations can be rough; the writer need not be an artist. The magazine maintains an artist on staff.

"Articles that are of historical content or make reference to previously published accounts should have a complete bibliography.

"New authors (not previously published extensively) are given some preference and encouragement to submit to *Whispering Wind*."

(Cross-reference: Native American)

Apache, Jicarilla
JICARILLA CHIEFTAIN
Editors: M.F. Polanco and V.L. Vigil
P.O. Box 507
Dulce
New Mexico 87528-0507
(505) 759-3242
Pub.: Jicarilla Apache Tribe
Established 1961
Sub.: U.S.:(in-co.$12; out-co.: $28); Intl.:$24
Distribution: Biweekly
Circulation: U.S.:1,100 total
English, some Jicarilla text
.06% non-English
Freelance articles accepted

SASE: Not indicated
No ms.language preferred
Query,letter only
No ms.length indicated
No payment
Photos/credits
Tabloid
Size:5 col.wide x 13"long
Black/white/color
Regular paper used
Paper color: Unknown
Display, classified
Deadline: Mon.aft.pub.
Univ/col.libs.,pols.
No "kill" fee

Jicarilla Chieftain publishes information on Jicarilla Apaches, other news which would have an impact on the people and the region, and national news of Native Americans.

The editors describe the contents as containing information which will inform, educate and enhance the life style of the readership.

For contributors, the editors prefer "timely information on Native American issues that will be of interest to our readers."

(Cross-referenced: Jicarilla.)

Arab, Muslim
ARAMCO WORLD
Editor: Robert Arndt
P.O. Box 4534
Houston
Texas 77210
(713) 432-4425
Publisher: Aramco
Established 1951
Sub.: U.S.:$0 (Controlled)
Distribution: Bimonthly
Cir.: U.S.:135,000; Intl.:30,000
English text
0% non-English
Freelance articles accepted

SASE: Not required
English ms.preferred
Query, letter
No ms.length indicated
Payment
Photos/credits/pay
Magazine
Size: 8.5" x 11"
Black/white/color
Glossy paper
White color paper
No advertising
Deadline: Not listed
Jour.,libraries, others
Pays "kill" fee

Aramco World is described by the editor as providing coverage of the history, culture, geography and economics of the Arab and Muslim world.

This magazine is received by many libraries and is widely read by journalists and other persons interested in oil and the Middle East.

Freelance articles and ideas are used. Authors are paid a flat fee if their contributions are used by Aramco World. If the idea is used but not the article, the author is paid a "kill" fee. The amount of the fee is determined at the editor's discretion.

Freelance photos are used; credits and payment are given. The fee for use of freelance photos is determined by agreement with the photographer or on a space-rate basis.

For writers, the editor looks for a balance between writings from within the Middle East and from outside the area. Authors should keep in mind that the readership is open-minded, but not well-informed on the subject.

The editor writes, "If there is any 'gee-whiz,' it had better come from the subject, not from the writing."

(Cross-referenced: Muslim.)

Arab-American
ARAB STUDIES QUARTERLY
Editor: Samih K.Farsoun
556 Trapelo Road
Belmont
Massachusetts 02178
(617) 484-5483
Pub.: Assoc.Arab-Amer U.Grad.Inc.
Established 1979
Sub.: U.S.:$16; Intl.:$20; Inst.:$35
Distribution: Quarterly
Circ.: U.S.:1,500; Intl.:300
English text
0% non-English
Freelance articles accepted
SASE: No response
English ms.preferred
Query unnecessary
No ms.length indicated
No payment
No photos
Format: No response
Size: Not listed
Black/white
Paper type: Not listed
Ivory color paper
Display
Deadline: 15th Feb.,May,Aug.,Nov.
Socio.,Econ.,political scientists
No "kill" fee

The Arab Studies Quarterly publishes scholarly studies of the politics, economy, history, society and culture of the Middle East, with an emphasis on the Arab world and related subjects.

The editors say that they assume responsibility for the selection of articles, but emphasize that authors are responsible for facts, interpretation and opinions expressed in their articles.

This periodical is received by institutions of higher learning and governmental agencies, as well as subscribers who are interested in Middle East studies and current events, such as sociologists, economists, political scientists, historians, ethnographers and others.

Arab-American
NEWS CIRCLE, THE
Editor: Joseph Haiek
P.O.Box 3684
6730 San Fernando Road
Glendale, California 91201
(818) 545-0333
Pub.: The News Circle Pub.House
Established June 1972
Subscription: U.S.:$20; Intl.:$65
Distribution: Monthly
Cir.: Contl.:3,500; Sub.:1,500
English, Arabic text
15% Arabic
Freelance articles accepted

SASE: Required
No ms.lang.preference
Query: No prefer.;letter o.k.
No ms.length indicated
No payment
Photos: Staff assigned
Magazine
Size: 8.5" x 11"
Black/white/color
Glossy and newsprint
White color paper
Display, classified
Deadline: 20th each month
Public libraries receive
No "kill" fee

The News Circle serves the Arab-American community by providing news of social, political, business, culture, the press/media, view and news of Arab-Americans and the Arab world.

For contributors, the editor says, "This publication does not have a healthy budget to spend on photos and articles. We receive more material than we can use, and it is free."

Armenian
ARMENIAN REPORTER, THE
Editor: Edward K. Bogosian
P.O.Box 600
Fresh Meadows
New York 11365
(718) 380-3636
Publisher: A.R. Publishing Corporation
Established 1967
Sub.: U.S.:$35; Intl.:$45(surface);$80(air)
Distribution: Weekly
Circulation: U.S.:5,000; Intl.:200
English text
% non-English: No response
Freelance articles accepted

SASE: Not required
English ms.preferred
Query, letter
No ms.length indicated
Payment, flat fee
Photos/credits
Tabloid
Size: 15" x 10"
Black/white
Newsprint paper
White color paper
Display ads
Deadline: Monday
Non-Armenians,govt.
No "kill" fee

The Armenian Reporter reports on almost every major news occurrence which relates to the Armenian communities in the United States and worldwide.

Among the non-ethnic group readers, the editors say some readers are non-Armenians married to Armenians and some are workers in governmental agencies.

The paper is described as serving as a platform for articles about community activities, views and opinions and letters to the editor.

The editor requests advance discussion of the subjects to be covered in any article submitted, and the discussion must be with the editor.

Armenian
CALIFORNIA COURIER
Editor: Harut Sassounian
P.O. Box 5390
Glendale
California 91201
(818) 409-0949
Publisher: Harut Sassounian
Established 1958
Sub: U.S.:$25; Intl.:$100(air mail)
Distribution: Weekly
Circulation: U.S.:2,900; Intl.:100
English text
0% non-English
Freelance articles accepted

SASE: Not required
English ms.preferred
Query: Not required
No ms.length indicated
Payment, flat fee
Photos accepted/credits
Newspaper/tabloid
Size: 11" x 14"
Black/white
Newsprint paper
White color paper
Display, classified
Deadline: Thursdays
Embassies, govt.,univ.
No "kill" fee

California Courier, as described by the editor, covers news of interest to the Armenian community, especially the California community, as well as national and international Armenian news items.

Among the non-ethnic group readers, *California Courier* is read by government officials, politicians and people at foreign embassies, universities and research centers.

The editorial content is described as defending the political, social and human rights of Armenians worldwide and exposing those who act against these interests.

The editor asks that contributors submit articles with an Armenian angle.

Armenian
NAVASART Monthly
Editor: Armen Donoyan
204 East Chevy Chase; Suite 6
Glendale
California 91205
(818) 241-5933
Publisher: Navasart Foundation
Established August 1982
Subscription: U.S.:$25; Intl.:$45
Distribution: Monthly
Circulation: U.S.:1,250; Intl.:90
Armenian, English text
80% non-English
Freelance articles accepted

SASE: Required
Armenian ms.preferred
Query unnecessary
No ms.length indicated
No pay freelance
Photos/credits
Magazine
Size: 11" x 8.5"
Black/white
Regular paper, offset
White color paper
Display ads accepted
Deadline: Not listed
No outside group readers
No "kill" fee

The ethnic interests of *NAVASART Monthly* are described in relation to the language used in the text of the periodical. It is the only Armenian language magazine published in the USA; as such it represents the Armenian heritage in the United States.

With respect to the editorial content of this periodical, the editor says the editorials describe all aspects of Armenian literature. The editor writes also that contributors to *NAVASART Monthly* feel proud and honored to have their articles and photographs published in the magazine.

Asian, Hispanic
EASTSIDE SUN
Editor: John Sanchez
2912 E. Brooklyn Ave.
Los Angeles
California 90033
(213) 263-5743
Publisher: Delores Sanchez
Established 1945
Sub.: U.S.:$29.50; Intl.:$29.50+postage
Distribution: Weekly
Circulation: U.S./Intl.:13,600
Spanish, English text
30% Spanish; 70% English
Freelance articles accepted

SASE: No response
No ms.lang.preference
Query: No response
Ms.lgth.: 2 pgs.or less
No pay for freelance
Photos/credits/no pay
Newspaper
Size: 13" x 21"
Black/white/color
Newsprint paper
White color paper
Display, classified
Deadline: Fri.week before pub.
Corp.leaders,Govt.,etc.
No "kill" fee

Eastside Sun publishes information on local or national news of interest to the Hispanic community. According to the editor, some Asian readers also receive *Eastside Sun*, so editors include some Asian news. The newspaper is described as "very democratic."

The editor suggests that contributors limit submissions to two pages or shorter as space is at a premium.

(Cross-referenced: Hispanic.)

Asian-American
CINEVUE
Editor: Bill J. Gee
32 E. Broadway; 4th Floor
New York
New York 10002
(212) 925-8685
Pub.: Asian CineVision, Inc.
Established: Date not listed
Sub.: U.S.; Intl.rates:Not listed
Distribution: Quarterly
Circulation: U.S.:15,000
English text
0% non-English
Freelance not accepted/staff assigned

SASE: Not applicable
English ms.preference
Query, letter
No ms.length indicated
Pay freelance/flat fee
Photos, credits, pay
Newspaper/tabloid
Size: Not listed
Black/white/color
Paper: 56 lb. weight
White color paper
Display
Deadline: Not listed
Outside group readers
No "kill" fee

CineVue is, according to the editor, a publication for an audience interested in Asian-American arts, culture, film and video. The editorial content contains features on cinema and video. Readers from outside the specific group are described as those who have similar interests in film and video works.

No freelance articles are accepted.

Asian-American
JADE, The Asian-American Magazine
No forwarding address
Old address:
Box 291367
Los Angeles, California 90029

The survey questionnaire was returned due to no forwarding address.

Asian-Am.,Black,Ethnic Studies,Hispanic,Nat.Am.
EQUAL OPPORTUNITY MAGAZINE
Editor: James Schneider
44 Broadway
Greenlawn
New York 11740
(516) 261-8917
Pub.: Equal Opportunity Pub.,Inc.
Established 1969
Subscription: U.S.:$13/yr.
Distribution: Three times/yr.
Circulation: U.S.:15,000 (controlled)
English text
0% non-English
Freelance articles accepted

SASE: Required
English ms.prefer
Query, letter
No ms.length listed
Pay by word
Photos/credits/pay
Magazine
Size: 8" x 10"
Black/white/color
Glossy paper
White paper
Display, classified
Deadline:6wk.b.pub.
College adm.
"Kill" fee: Unknown

The editor says about *Equal Opportunity Magazine*: "Our magazine is received by college students and young professionals who are Black, Hispanic, Native American and Asian-American. The focus is on career-guidance and job information."

This magazine provides role-model profiles, career-guidance topics and news of career opportunities for minorities.

The editors encourage writers to target articles specifically for the audience just described. Writers should present well-written, clean and professional manuscripts. Please include cover letter which details writing experience.

Those who wish to place either display or classified ads must submit the ad materials six weeks prior to desired publication date.

(Cross-referenced: Black, Ethnic Studies, Hispanic, Native American.)

Asian-American, Japanese
PACIFIC CITIZEN
Acting Editor:J.K. Yamamoto
941 East 3rd. St.; No.200
Los Angeles
California 90013
(213) 626-6936
Pub.: Japanese American Citizens League
Established 1929
Subscription: U.S.:$20; Intl.:$32
Distribution: Weekly
Circulation: U.S.:23,800; Intl.:120
English text
0% non-English
Freelance articles accepted

SASE: Required
English ms.preferred
Query, letter
No ms.lgth.indicated
Payment, flat fee
Photo/credits/flat fee
Tabloid
Size: Not listed
Black/white
Newsprint paper
White color paper
Display, classified
Deadline: Mon.bef.pub.
Libs.,mem.of Congress
No "kill" fee

Pacific Citizen contains Asian-American community news with an emphasis on the Japanese American community. In addition to the ethnic group readers, there are libraries and politicians, including members of Congress, who receive the periodical.

The editor writes that *Pacific Citizen* publishes news articles on civil rights issues such as redress for Japanese Americans interned during World War II, violence against Asian-Americans, job discrimination, university admissions of Asian-Americans and other subjects of related interest. Feature sections focus on trends in Japanese-American communities, interesting personalities, such as politicians, artists and others, activities of Japanese American Citizens League, calendar items on upcoming community events, various columns and reviews.

For contributors the editor writes, "Recommend looking over sample issues first to get an idea of content and format. Some familiarity with Japanese American or general Asian-American community, history and current issues (is) needed."

(Cross-referenced: Japanese.)

Assyrian-American
ASSYRIAN STAR
S. Abraham
Old address:
Assyrian-American Federation
Box 59309
Chicago, Illinois 60659

The survey questionnaire was returned due to no forwarding address.

B

Basque
ANGLO-AMERICAN BASQUE STUDIES NEWSLETTER

The *Anglo-American Basque Studies Newsletter* is no longer published, but was published at the University of Nevada by the Basque Studies Program; Reno, Nevada, 89557.

Basque
BASQUE STUDIES NEWSLETTER
Editor: William A. Douglass
University of Nevada Library
Reno
Nevada 89557
(702) 784-4854
Publisher: Basque Studies Program
Established November 1968
Subscription: U.S.: Free/Controlled
Distribution: Biennial
Cir.: U.S.:7,900; Intl.:600
English, occasional Basque text
% non-English: Minimal
No freelance/Staff assigned

SASE: No response
Ms.lang.: No response
No queries accepted
No ms.length indicated
No payment
No photos
Newsletter
Size: 8.5" x 6.5"
Black/white print
Regular paper
White color paper
No ads
Deadline: Not listed
Univ./pub.libraries;Basque interests
"Kill" fee: No response

The ethnic interests of the *Basque Studies Newsletter* are described as Basque. The non-ethnic groups that receive the newsletter are university and public libraries within Basque-populated areas.

The *Basque Studies Newsletter* has an academic orientation with news of activities of the Basque Studies Program staff and other researchers in the field. There are one or two articles of general interest on Basque-related topics in each publication.

Although articles from scholars in the study area are published occasionally, the publisher doesn't solicit contributions because they are not budgeted to pay for the articles.

Bengali
SANGBAD BICHITRA
Editor: R.K. Datta
101 Iden Ave.
Pelham Manor
New York 10803
(914) 738-5727
Pub.: Cultural Assoc.of Bengal
Established 1971
Subscription: U.S.:$12; Intl.:$20
Distribution: Once every 3 weeks
Circulation: U.S.:1,000; Intl.:10
Bengali text
100% non-English
Freelance articles accepted

SASE: Not required
No ms.lang.preference
Query: No preference
No ms.length indicated
No payment
Photos/credits
Tabloid
Size: 11" x 16"
Black/white
Newsprint paper
White color paper
Display, classified
Deadline: Not listed
No outside group readers
No "kill" fee

The Cultural Association of Bengal publishes *Sangbad Bichitra* once every three weeks in the Bengali language.

The editor lists no tips for contributors.

As with most publications, writers who wish to contribute, would probably benefit from reviewing the publication prior to submitting a manuscript to the editor for consideration in publication.

Black
AFRICAN-AMERICAN TRAVELER NEWSLETTER,THE
Editor: Linda Cousins
P.O. Box 5; Radio City Station
New York
New York 10101-0005
(718) 774-4379
Publisher: Universal Black Writer Press
Established 1987
Subscription: U.S.:$16; Intl.:$20
Distribution: Quarterly
Circulation: Total: 500
English text
0% non-English
Freelance articles accepted

SASE: Required
English ms.prefer
Query: Phone/ltr.
No ms.lgth. indic.
Pay: Flat fee
Photos/crs./pay
Newsletter
Size: 8.5" x 11"
Black/white
Paper type: Unk.
White color paper
Display, classified
Deadline: Not indic.
No outside gp.rdrs.
"Kill" fee: Unknown

The African-American Traveler Newsletter is written for culturally-aware Black travelers who desire to support and enjoy Black businesses and entertainment worldwide, according to editor and publisher Linda Cousins.

Cousins writes that the newsletter contains travel research information and articles geared to identifying interesting, high-quality

Black travel-related businesses in the Caribbean and Africa, and encourages the support of Black businesses worldwide.

The African-American Traveler Newsletter contains feature articles on international Black historical sites, Black artistic and cultural events, where to buy crafts and artwork by Black residents, and much more about Black-owned hotels, guest houses, inns, nightspots and restaurants.

For the prospective contributor, Cousins writes, "Travel articles on Black-owned business/culture in Africa and the Caribbean, although articles on such in other countries are also welcome."

Short reviews on the literature of the Caribbean and Africa, as well as, interesting accounts of personal travel experiences are considered.

Sample copies of the newsletter cost $4.00.

Black
BLACK FAMILY
Old address:
P.O. Box 16940
Chicago
Illinois 60616

Black Family is no longer published according to information from the publication's executive office.

Black
BLACK NEWS
Old address:
186 Remsen Street
Brooklyn, New York 11201.

The survey questionnaire was returned due to no forwarding address.

Black
BLACK SCHOLAR, THE
Editors: R.Chrisman or J.Abron
P.O.Box 2869
Oakland
California 94609
(415) 547-6633
Publisher: Robert Chrisman
Established September 1969
Sub.: U.S.Ind.$25;Inst.$35;Intl.:+$6
Distribution: Bimonthly
Circulation: U.S.:Unlisted; Intl:150
English text
0% non-English
Freelance articles accepted
SASE: Required
English ms.preference
Query: Telephone/letter
No ms.length indicated
No payment
Staff assigned photos
Magazine
Size: 7" x 10"
Black/white
Paper type: No response
Color: Not white/buff
Display, classified
Deadline: 10th of odd mo.
Coll.& univ.libraries
No "kill" fee

The Black Scholar is a journal of Black Studies and Research.

No other information was provided.

Black
CRISES (NEW YORK)
F. Beauford
Old address:
186 Remsen Street
Brooklyn, New York 11201.

The survey questionnaire was returned due to no forwarding address.

Black
DELAWARE VALLEY DEFENDER
Editor: A.G. Hibbert
1702 Locust Street
Wilmington
Delaware 19802
(302) 656-3252
Publisher: Defender Publishing Co., Inc.
Established 1962
Subscription: U.S.:$15
Distribution: Weekly
Circulation: U.S.:13,000
English text
0% non-English
Freelance articles:No response

SASE: No response
English ms.preference
Query: No response
No ms.length indicated
No payment
Photos/credits/no pay
Newspaper
Size: Not listed
Black/white/color
Newsprint paper
White color paper
Display, classified
Deadline: Friday
No outside group readers
"Kill" fee: No response

According to *Ulrich's International Directory of Periodicals*, this newspaper, *Delaware Valley Defender*, focuses on the Black interests of the community it serves. The editor did not provide information relative to the ethnic interests of the newspaper.

Black
LINCOLN REVIEW
Editor: J.A. Parker
Old address:
1735 De Sales St.N.W.; 8th Floor
Washington, D.C. 20036

The survey questionnaire was returned due to no forwarding address.

Black
MAINSTREAM AMERICA MAGAZINE
D. Clark
Old address:
2417 W. Vernon Ave.
Los Angeles, California 90008.

The survey questionnaire was returned due to no forwarding address.

Black
OBSERVER NEWSPAPERS, THE
Editor: William H. Lee
3540-4th Avenue
Sacramento
California 95801
(916) 425-4781
Publisher: William H. Lee
Established November 1962
Subscription: No fee given
Distribution: Weekly
Circulation: 97,000 total
English text
0% non-English
Freelance articles accepted
SASE: No response
English ms.preference
Query, letter
No ms.length indicated
No payment
Photos/credits
Newspaper
Size: 10" x 15"
Black/white/color
Newsprint paper
White color paper
Display, classified
Deadline: Tues.each week
About 30% non-Black readers
"Kill" fee: Not applicable

The Observer Newspapers are three Black community newspapers with full comprehensive coverage of the Black community. The newspapers provide news of interest on and about the Black experience locally, nationally and internationally. For contributors, the editor writes, "Please feel free to submit materials, articles and others to us. We serve the Black communities of Northern California."

Black
PROUD MAGAZINE
Editor: Betty Lee
625 No. Euclid Ave; Suite 200
St. Louis
Missouri 63108
(314) 361-7877
Publisher: Proud, Inc.
Established 1969
Subscription: U.S.:$5
Distribution: Quarterly
Cir.: U.S.:l0,000; Intl.:0
English text
0% non-English
No freelance accepted/Staff assigned
SASE: Not applicable
English manuscript preference
Query:No preference/letter o.k.
No manuscript length indicated
No payment
Photos staff assigned
Magazine
Size: 8.5" x 11"
Black/white;color cover
Glossy paper
White color paper
Display
Deadline: 30 days before pub.
Colleges,universities,others
"Kill" fee: No response

The ethnic interests of *Proud Magazine* are described by the editor as focusing on the "Black perspective" with the editorial content aimed at Black advocacy.

Black
SUN-REPORTER
Editor: Carlton B. Goodlett
1366 Turk Street
San Francisco
California 94115
(415) 931-5778
Publisher: Thomas C.Fleming
Established 1943
Subscription: U.S.:$11 (Controlled)
Distribution: Weekly
Circulation: U.S.:11,500
English text
0% non-English
Freelance maybe acc./Mostly staff assigned

SASE: No response
English manuscript preferred
Query: Not applicable
No ms. length indicated
Pay for freelance
Photos accepted/pay
Tabloid
Size: Not listed
Black/white/color
Newsprint paper
White color paper
Display, classified
Deadline: Not listed
Outside group readers
Pays "kill" fee

The editor of *Sun-Reporter* describes the editorial content as "liberal." With respect to articles published, the editor writes that articles are staff assigned, but, if a freelance idea is used, a "kill" fee is paid, and, if an article submitted by a freelance writer is used, the writer is paid by the column inch and/or the news story.

According to the response on the questionnaire, there are readers outside the ethnic-interest group, but the editor does not indicate who these readers are.

Black
WESTERN JOURNAL OF BLACK STUDIES
Editor: Talmadge Anderson
Heritage House; Black Studies Program
Washington State University
Pullman, Washington 99164-3310
(509) 335-8681
Pub.: Black Studies Program/WSU
Established March 1977
Sub.: U.S.:$15; Canada:$15; Institutions:$22
Distribution: Quarterly
Circulation: Not given
English text
0% non-English
Freelance scholarly articles accepted

SASE: No response
English ms.preference
Query WSU Press editor
Ms.length: Max.:28 pages
Pay: No information
Photos with manuscripts
Magazine
Size: 8" x 10"
Black/white
Glossy paper
White color paper
Ads accepted if academic
Deadline: Not listed
Unk. outside gp.readers
"Kill" fee: No response

The *Western Journal of Black Studies* is an interdisciplinary periodical which publishes monographs about research, social analysis, political commentary, literary criticism and contemporary arts.

According to the information sheet which accompanied sample

copies of the *Western Journal of Black Studies*, the editors invite contributions from "Afro-American writers and others who have a profound and scholarly interest in the universal Black experience." Contributions from international writers and artists are invited as well.

Authors who plan to submit a manuscript are encouraged to obtain manuscript guidelines prior to submitting the paper.

Black,Ethnic Studies,Hispanic,Nat.Am.,Asian-Am.	SASE: Required
EQUAL OPPORTUNITY MAGAZINE	Eng.ms.preferred
Editor: James Schneider	Query, letter
44 Broadway	No ms.length listed
Greenlawn	Pay by word
New York 11740	Photos/credits/pay
(516) 261-8917	Magazine
Pub.: Equal Opportunity Pub.,Inc.	Size: 8" x 10"
Established 1969	Black/white/color
Subscription: U.S.:$13/yr.	Glossy paper
Distribution: Three times/yr.	White paper
Circulation: U.S.:15,000 (Controlled)	Display, classified
English text	Deadline:6wks.b.pub.
0% non-English	Coll.administrators
Freelance articles accepted	"Kill" fee: Unknown

The editor says about *Equal Opportunity Magazine*: "Our magazine is received by college students and young professionals who are Black, Hispanic, Native American and Asian-American. The focus is on career-guidance and job information."

This magazine provides role model profiles, career guidance topics and news of career opportunities for minorities.

The editors encourage writers to target articles specifically for the audience just described. Writers should present well-written, clean and professional manuscripts. Please include cover letter which details writing experience.

Those who wish to place either display or classified ads must submit the ad materials six weeks prior to desired publication date.

(Cross-referenced: Asian-American, Ethnic studies, Hispanic, Native American.)

Black, Hispanic
AIM MAGAZINE
Editor: Ruth Apilado
7308 So. Eberhart
Chicago
Illinois 60619
(312) 874-6184
Publisher: Ruth Apilado
Established January 1974
Sub.: U.S.:$8; International:$10
Distribution: Quarterly
Cir.: U.S.:8,000; Controlled:4,000
English text
0% non-English
Freelance articles accepted

SASE: No response
English manuscript preference
Query unnecessary
No manuscript length indicated
Payment
Photo/credits/no pay
Magazine
Size: 8" x 11.5"
Black/white
Newsprint paper
White color paper
Display
Deadline: 15th of M.,Je.,Sep.,Dec.
Colleges,universities,gen.public
No "kill" fee

Aim Magazine is described by the editor as follows: "We're interested in promoting racial harmony and peace--in correcting false racial opinions of the majority--building confidence and pride in black and Hispanic Americans--all through the written word. Often we select an unknown in a community and profile him/her, who is making a contribution to social progress."

With respect to tips to contributors, the editor says that contributors should look for an event that has made a great contribution toward solving racial problems.

(Cross-referenced: Hispanic.)

Black-American
CALL AND POST
Editor: John Genear
1949 East 105th Street
Cleveland
Ohio 44106
(216) 791-7600
Publisher: P.W. Publishing Company,Inc.
Established 1915
Subscription: U.S.:$12 (Controlled)
Distribution: Weekly
Circulation: U.S.:47,000
English text
0% non-English
Freelance articles accepted

SASE: No response
English ms.prefer
No ms.length indicated
Query, letter
Payment
Photos/credits
Newspaper
Size: Not listed
Black/white print
Newsprint paper
White color paper
Display, classified
Deadline: Tuesday
Outside group readers
Pays "kill" fee

The *Call and Post* is a Black-oriented newspaper.

Black-American
EM: EBONY MAN MAGAZINE
Editor: Alfred Fonray
1270 Ave.of Americas; 26th floor
New York
New York 10020
(212) 397-4555
Publisher: Johnson Publishing Co.
Established November 1985
Subscription: Fee not listed
Distribution: Monthly
Circulation: U.S.:251,000; Intl.:30,000
English text
0% non-English
Freelance articles accepted

SASE: No response
English manuscript preferred
Query: Letter
No manuscript length indicated
Sometimes pay
Photos/pay/credits
Magazine
Size: Not listed
Black/white/color
Glossy paper
White color paper
Display
Deadline: Unknown
Outside group readers
No "kill" fee

EM: Ebony Man Magazine is, according to the editor, published for a special market: Black men. The articles published focus on fashion, grooming, health and fitness.

No other tips were provided for freelance contributors.

Black-American
FACTS NEWSPAPER, THE
Editor: Fitzgerald Beaver
2765 E. Cherry
Seattle
Washington 98122
(206) 324-0552
Publisher: Fitzgerald Beaver
Established 1962
Subscription: U.S.:$40
Distribution: Weekly
Sub.: U.S.:35,000; Controlled:5,000
English text
0% non-English
Freelance articles accepted

SASE: Required
English manuscript preferred
Query unnecessary
No manuscript lgth.indicated
No payment
Photos/credits/no pay
Format: Not listed
Size: 10" x 21"
Black/white print
Newsprint paper
White color paper
Display, classified
Deadline: Monday noon
Some outside group readers
No "kill" fee

The Facts Newspaper is a periodical with a local focus on Black minority news and is published in Seattle, Washington.

The editor writes that freelance articles and photographs are accepted. No payment is given for either articles or photographs.

Writers and photographers are encouraged to review a copy of the newspaper before submitting materials.

Black-American	SASE: Required
MILWAUKEE COURIER NEWSPAPER	English ms.preference
Editor: Marva Pattillo	Query necessary
2431 West Hopkins Street	No ms.length indicated
Milwaukee	Payment negotiated
Wisconsin 53206	Photos/cr./pay negotiated
(414) 449-4860	Newspaper
Pub.: Milwaukee Courier Newspaper	Size: Not listed
Established June 1963	Black/white/color
Subscription: U.S.:$9.50	Newsprint paper
Distribution: Weekly	Buff color paper
Circulation: U.S.:15,000	Display, classified
English text	Deadline: Not listed
0% non-English	No outside group readers
Freelance articles accepted	No "kill" fee

The *Milwaukee Courier Newspaper* audience is described as Black Americans.

The editor provided no other descriptions concerning the content of the newspaper and no contributor's tips.

Black-American, African	SASE: Required
BLACK AMERICAN LITERATURE FORUM	No ms.lang.preferred
Eds.: Joe Weixlmann, Carole Gustafson	Query with SASE
Indiana State University	No ms.lgth.indicated
Parsons Hall	Pay: Copies
Terre Haute, Indiana 47809	Photos/credits/no pay
(812) 237-3169	Magazine
Publisher: Indiana St. University	Size: 6" x 9"
Established 1967	Black/white
Sub.: U.S.:$15/21; Intl.:$18/21(ind./inst.)	Regular paper
Distribution: Quarterly	Buff color paper
Cir.: U.S.:1,045;International:69 (Contl./sub.)	No ads; considering
English text	Deadline: Unknown
0% non-English	Some colleges subscribe
Freelance articles accepted	No "kill" fee listed

The *Black American Literature Forum* is described as a publisher of "belletristic" writing, that is, literature which addresses the aesthetic rather than offering didactic or informative content. The editors indicate an occasional interest in Black American art, film, music and the writing of non-American Blacks. Also, essays on Black American literature, art and culture, bibliographies, interviews, poems and book reviews are published.

Before articles are selected for publication in the *Black American Literature Forum*, the articles are reviewed by a twenty-member editorial board of nationally-recognized experts in the field of Black American literature and culture. The editorial board thoroughly reviews manuscripts for content, subject treatment by the author and style.

The editors provided no tips for contributors.

Prospective contributors would probably benefit from obtaining a copy of the periodical before submitting manuscripts for review.

Authors are provided with 11 copies of the published article as a form of payment.

(Cross-referenced: African.)

British
U.K. MAGAZINE
Editor: Mary D. Griffiths
111 Clayton Road
Hatboro
Pennsylvania 19040
(215) 674-3132
Publisher: Mary D. Griffiths
Established 1982
Subscription: U.S.:$12; Intl.:$16
Distribution: Bimonthly
Circulation: U.S.:24,000; Intl.:200
English text
0% non-English
Freelance articles accepted
SASE: No response
English manuscript preferred
Query: Phone, letter
No manuscript length indicated
Pay: Sometimes
Photos/credits/pay occas.
Magazine
Size: 8" x 11"
Black/white/color
Glossy paper
White color paper
Display, classified
Deadline: 1 month before publication
Outside group readers
"Kill" fee sometimes paid

U.K.Magazine publishes articles with a British Isles heritage focus.

No contributor's tips were provided.

Byelorussian
BIELARUS
Editor: Jan Zaprudnik
166-34 Gothic Drive
Jamaica
New York 11432
(212) 397-5341
Pub.: The Byelorussian-American Assoc., Inc.
Established 1951
Subscription: U.S./Intl.:$15/year
Distribution: Monthly
Circulation: U.S.:1,500; Intl.:500
Byelorussian text
100% non-English
Freelance articles accepted

SASE : No response
No ms.language prefer
Query: No response
No ms.length indicated
No payment
Photo/credits/no pay
Tabloid
Size: Not listed
Black/white
Paper: No response
White color paper
Ads.: No response
Deadline: No response
Libraries, scholars
"Kill" fee: No response

Bielarus is described as a link between Byelorussian communities in the Western world and a provider of information on happenings in Soviet Byelorussia, which the editor described as "struggle for national survival and the development of Byelorussian culture and resistance to 'russification.'"

The editor indicates that plans are being made to introduce an English language page.

The editor writes that the periodical "tries to show unknown or distorted facts of Byelorussian history, to report on attempts to creatively develop Byelorussian culture, to denounce attempts to stifle or falsify facts of Byelorussian presence, to report on the life of Byelorussians in the West, and generally support democracy, freedom and mutual understanding in all nations."

C

Carpatho-Rusyn
CARPATHO-RUSYN AMERICANS
Editor: John Haluska
P.O.Box 227
Cambridge
Minnesota 55008
(612) 689-1720
Pub.: Carpatho-Rusyn Research Center
Established 1978
Subscription: U.S.:$12; Intl.:$12
Distribution: Quarterly
Circulation: U.S.:900; Intl.:100
English and East European text
5% or less non-English
Freelance articles accepted

SASE: Not required
English ms.preference
Query unnecessary
No ms.length indicated
Sometimes pay
Photos/cr./sometimes pay
Magazine
Size: 8.5" x 11"
Black/white/color
Regular paper
White color paper
Ads: Not indicated
Deadline: Not listed
Outside group readers
No "kill" fee

Carpatho-Rusyn American is a periodical for Carpatho-Rusyn Americans. The publication is printed primarily in English, although Carpatho-Rusyn, Ukrainian, Russian, Polish and Slovak languages are sometimes used.

The magazine is described by the editor as "non-political" and "non-religious."

Compensation is sometimes given for freelance articles and photos. The editor noted that compensation for photos is "perhaps negotiable."

Celtic, Irish, Scottish, Welsh
THE DRAGON, THE THISTLE, THE HARP
Editor: J.D. Holsinger
2214 E. Cherryvale
Springfield
Missouri 65804
No phone listing
Pub.: Celtic Society of Missouri Ozarks
Established 1987
Subscription: Rate not listed
Distribution: Quarterly
Circulation: U.S.:50
English text
%non-English: Minimal
Freelance accepted: Editor's decision

SASE: No response
Ms.lang.: Not listed
Query, letter
No ms.length indicated
Pay policy: Not listed
Photos: No response
Newsletter
Size: 8.5" x 11" or 16"
Black/white
Bond paper
White color paper
No ads accepted
Deadline: Not listed
No outside group readers
"Kill" fee: No response

The Dragon, The Thistle, The Harp is a publication which, according to the editor, "tries to have articles on the Welsh, Scottish and Irish, especially in Missouri."

A sample copy of *The Dragon, The Thistle, The Harp* contained articles about significant events, origin of Celtic names in the Ozarks, a pronunciation technique discussion and news about members of the Celtic Society of Missouri Ozarks.

The editor writes that he has had no experience with people "sending articles" (to him for possible publication).

(Cross-referenced: Irish, Scottish, Welsh.)

Chicano	SASE: No response
AZTLAN	No ms.lang.preference
Editor: Candelyn Candelaria	Query not required
405 Hilgard Avenue	No ms.length indicated
Univ.of California-Los Angeles	No payment
Los Angeles, California 90024	Photos/credits/no pay
(213) 825-2642	Academic journ.format
Pub.: Chicano Studies Research Center, UCLA	Size: Not listed
Established 1970	Black/white/color
Sub.: U.S.:$15-20; Intl.:$26	Bond paper
Distribution: Biannual	White color paper
Circulation: U.S.:475; Intl.:25	No advertising
Spanish and English text	Deadline: Not listed
%non-English not indicated	Research institutions
Freelance articles accepted	"Kill" fee: Not appl.

Aztlan is published by the Chicano Studies Research Center, University of California-Los Angeles (UCLA), and is described as an academic journal with a Chicano focus.

The editor suggests contributors adhere to submission guidelines for manuscripts which can be found in the latest issue of the journal.

Chicano, Latino
EL TECOLOTE NEWSPAPER
Editor: Carlos Alcala
P.O. Box 40037
San Francisco
California 94140
(415) 824-7878
Publisher: Accion Latina
Established August 1970
Sub.: U.S.Individual:$8; Institution:$30
Distribution: Monthly
Circulation: U.S.:10,000
Spanish, English text
50% non-English (approximately)
Freelance articles accepted

SASE for ms.return
No ms.lang.preference
Query, letter
No ms.length indicated
No payment
Photos/credits/no pay
Tabloid
Size: 10" x 16.5"
Black/white; one color
Newsprint paper
Paper color: Not listed
Display, classified
Deadline: Call for info.
Outside gp.rdrs.: Unknown
No "kill" fee

El Tecolote Newspaper focuses on the issues and culture of Chicanos and Latinos with some interest in other Third World cultures, such as the Philippines, Palestine, and other countries.

The editor says that the newspaper has a heavy emphasis on community issues and political questions at the national, international and regional levels which may affect the community. Some cultural reporting and analysis is included.

The editor's suggestions for contributors: "Know your technique; know your subject matter."

(Cross-referenced: Latino.)

Chinese-American
EAST/WEST NEWS
Editor: Richard Springer
838 Grant Avenue
San Francisco
California 94108
(415) 781-3194
Pub: East/West Chinese-American Journal Inc.
Established January 1967
Subscription: U.S.:$15; Intl: $25
Circulation: U.S.:15,000; Intl.:Few
Distribution: Weekly
Chinese, English text
20% non-English
Freelance articles accepted

SASE: Required
No ms.lang.preferred
Query, letter
No ms.length indicated
Payment
No photos accepted
Tabloid
Size: 11.5" x 15"
Black/white/color
Newsprint paper
White color paper
Display, classified
Deadline: Monday
Libs., government offices
No "kill" fee

The *East/West News* provides news, columns and entertainment for the Chinese-American community, as well as other news of interest to the readers, according to the editor of the periodical.

Among the outside groups who receive *East/West News*, the editors lists institutional libraries, government officials and friends of the Chinese American community.

The editor suggests that prospective contributors always read the paper before submitting articles for possible publication.

Choctaw Indian
CHOCTAW COMMUNITY NEWS
Editor: Julie Kelsey
Rt.7; Box 21
Philadelphia
Mississippi 39350
(601) 656-5251, ext.322
Pub.: Mississippi Band of Choctaw Indians
Established 1972
Subscription: No fees
Distribution: 10 times per year
Circulation: U.S.:3,025; Intl.:175
English, some Choctaw text
2% non-English
Freelance accepted, but seldom

SASE: No response
English ms.preferred
Query: No preference
No ms.lgth.indicated
No payment
Photos seldom accepted
Tabloid
Size: 11" x 14"
Black/white
Newsprint paper
White color paper
No advertising
Deadline: Not listed
Other tribes, libs.
"Kill" fee: N/A

The readers of *Choctaw Community News* are described as being concerned almost exclusively with news of interest to Choctaw Indians, with many copies sent to politicians, as well as college and university libraries. The newspaper occasionally includes general news articles about other tribes.

The newspaper contains a monthly commentary about tribal affairs written by the tribal chief and a report of his activities, general information about services offered by tribal administration, legislative activities by the tribal council and reservation news from community people.

Freelance photos are seldom accepted, but if accepted, photo credits are given if required.

For contributors, the editor writes, "Any freelance work about Mississippi Choctaws living elsewhere, done in feature form, would be of interest. Photographs should be included."

Croatian, Yugoslavian
ZAJEDNICAR (The Fraternalist)
Editor: Edward J. Verlich
100 Delaney Dr.
Pittsburgh
Pennsylvania 15235
(412) 351-3909
Pub.: Croatian Fraternal Union of America
Established 1904
Sub.: Controlled-Members only
Distribution: Weekly
Cir.: U.S.:33,000; Intl.:7,000
Croatian, English text
35-40% non-English
Freelance acceptance: Editor's decision

SASE: No response
English ms.preferred
Query: No response
No ms.length indicated
No payment
Photos/no pay
Tabloid
Size: 11.5" x 16.5"
Black/white/color
Newsprint paper
White color paper
No advertising
Deadline: Unknown
No outside readers
No "kill" fee paid

Zajednicar seeks to inform its membership of the events in the Croatian Fraternal Union of America. The periodical publishes information to help preserve and promote Croatian heritage and culture, keep the membership informed of the events in Croatia and Yugoslavia, promote Croatian art, music and culture, as well as encourage and publish events of the junior and adult tamburitza ensembles.

The editorial content contains news, human interest articles and feature stories with ample pictorial display of members, lodges, national officers, National Administration, central committees, junior and adult tamburitzans, Croatia and Yugoslavia.

The editor writes, "We reserve the right to edit, change, add and delete. You can contribute completed story or just give us the facts, and we'll do the rest."

(Cross-referenced: Yugoslavian.)

Cuban, Latin American, South American	SASE: Required
LA TRIBUNA DE NORTH JERSEY	Spanish ms.preference
Editor: Humberto Perez	Query, letter
70 Kossuth Street	No ms.length indicated
Newark	No payment
New Jersey 07101	Photos/credits/no pay
(201) 589-3742	Tabloid
Publisher: Carlos Bidot	Size: Not indicated
Established March 11, 1962	B/W; Color in spec.editions
Subscription: U.S.:$25 (Controlled)	Paper type: Not given
Distribution: Bimonthly	White color paper
Circulation: U.S.:50,000 Total	Display, classified
Spanish text	Deadline: Not listed
100% non-English	Colleges, businesses
Freelance articles accepted/Agent referred	No "kill" fee

La Tribuna de North Jersey publishes information for the Cuban exile community, Latin Americans and South Americans in the United States. The primary focus of the editorial content is human rights against dictatorship and against Communism.

The editor provided no "tips for contributors."

(Cross-referenced: Latin Americans and South Americans.)

Cypriot, Greek, Greek-American	SASE: Not required
AHEPAN	English ms.preference
Editor: Elias Valanton	Query unnecessary
1707 L St. NW; Suite 200	No ms.length indicated
Washington	Pay/flat fee
D.C. 20036	Photos: Staff assigned
(202) 628-4974	Magazine
Publisher: Ahepan	Size: Not listed
Established: 1928	Black/white/color
Subscription: U.S.:$10 (Controlled)	Glossy paper
Distribution: Quarterly	Color paper: Unknown
Cir.: U.S.:35,000; Intl.:2,000	Display
English text	Deadline: Not listed
5% non-English (less than)	No outside group readers
Freelance articles accepted	No "kill" fee

Ahepan publishes fraternal information and articles about Greece, Cyprus and Greek-American issues.

The editor of *Ahepan* did not provide any tips for contributors, but since freelance articles are accepted, contributors would probably benefit from reviewing a copy of the publication prior to submitting manuscripts for consideration.

(Cross-referenced: Greek and Greek-American.)

Czechoslovakian
HOSPODAR
Editor: Jerome Kopecky
Box 38
West
Texas 96691
(817) 826-3718
Publisher: Linn A. Pescaia
Established 1891
Subscription: U.S.:$14; Intl.:$17
Distribution: Monthly
Circulation: U.S.:1,163; Intl.:1,305
Czechoslovakian text
100% non-English
Freelance articles accepted

SASE: Required
Czech ms.preference
Query, letter
No ms.length indicated
No pay freelance
Photos accepted/credits
Tabloid
Size: 11.25" x 16"
Black/white
Newsprint paper
White paper color
Display, classified
Deadline: 15th of month
No outside group readers
No "kill" fee paid

Hospodar is a tabloid published monthly and contains information about Czech history, travelogues, letters, news, and so forth.

The editor had no tips for contributors.

D

Danish
AMERICAN DANE
Editor: Pamela K. Dorau
3717 Harney St.
Omaha
Nebraska 6813
(402) 341-5049
Pub.: Danish Brotherhood in America
Established February 1916
Sub.: U.S.:$6; Intl.:$8 (Controlled)
Distribution: Monthly
Circulation: U.S.:9,750; Intl.:250
English, Danish text
5% non-English
Freelance articles accepted

SASE: Required
No ms.language preference
Query, letter o.k.
No ms.length indicated
Payment/flat fee
Photos/credit/flat fee
Magazine
Size: 8.5" x 11"
Black/white/color
Glossy paper
White color paper
Display, classified
Deadline: 15th of mo.b.pub.
Clubs, libraries, colleges
No "kill" fee

American Dane is designed to help preserve and promote Danish heritage. The Danish Brotherhood offers numerous charitable and recreational activities nationally and through individual lodges and districts.

The editor listed no tips for contributors.

E

Estonian
ESTO AMERICA
Editors: Juta or Peeter Ristsoo
300 E. 91st. St. Street
New York
New York 10128
(212) 722-8581 or (212) 262-5655
Pub.: Esto America Publishing
Established December 1983
Sub.: U.S./Canada:$35; Intl.:$45
Distr.: Mo. and biannual newsletter
Circulation: U.S.:440; Intl.:150
Estonian, English text
20% non-English
Freelance articles accepted

SASE: Required
No ms.lang.preference
Query, letter
No ms.length indicated
No pay articles
Photos/credits/no pay
Magazine
Size: 8.5" x 11"
Black/white print
Newsprint & glossy paper
White & gray color paper
Display, classified
Deadline: May 30 & Nov.30
Libraries, govt. agencies
No "kill" fee

Esto America, as described by the editor, is written and published for the Estonian community in North America, with a secondary focus on Estonians worldwide.

Regarding the magazine's content, the editor writes, "(*Esto America*) covers the activities of the Estonian community in exile, that is, outside the Soviet Union, follows developments in Soviet Estonia, political analysis, first-person reports and news stories."

In addition to the monthly magazine, a biannual, glossy newsletter is published. Display and classified advertising deadlines are May 30th and Nov. 30th.

Ethnic Studies
BUILDING BLOCKS
Editor: John A. Kromkowski, Director
P.O. Box 20; Cardinal Station
Washington, D.C. 20064
(202) 232-3600
National Center for Urban Ethnic Affairs

Building Blocks, a publication of The National Center for Urban Ethnic Affairs (NCUEA), has suspended publication due to lack of funds, but the NCUEA maintains a working telephone, director and answers its mail.

Two samples of the publication *Building Blocks* (1981 and 1985) were provided with the completed questionnaire. This publication contained information about the work of the NCUEA, neighborhood culture, research and development, housing, research grants, and zoning policies to name a few of the areas of interest.

People interested in the work of the NCUEA should send query letters to the director for information. Also, The Catholic University of America; Department of Politics; Washington, D.C.; 20064. may be of some assistance.

Ethnic Studies
EMIE BULLETIN
Editor: David Cohen
Queens College, Sch.of Lib.Mg.Studies.
Kiely Hall, Rm.215
Flushing, New York 11367
(718) 520-7139 or 7194
Pub.: Ethnic Mat.Info.Exc.Rnd.Tbl.
Established 1983
Subscription: U.S.:$5; International:$5
Distribution: Quarterly
Circulation: U.S.:500;Intl.:100
English text
0% non-English
Freelance articles accepted

SASE: Required
English ms.preference
Query: Req./phone o.k.
No ms.length indicated
No payment
Photos/credits
Magazine
Size: 8.5" x 11"
Black/white
Regular bond paper
Gold and/or green paper
No advertising
Deadline: Not applicable
College & univ.libraries
No "kill" fee

EMIE Bulletin is multi-ethnic and multi-cultural in scope.

The editor writes, "We cover ALL minorities in the American pluralistic service, i.e., not (only) Black, Asian, Hispanic, American Indian, but Jews, Irish, Italian, Polish, etc.

"The *EMIE Bulletin* deals with the Round Table in Ethnic neo-trends in the American Library Association. We cover in-house organization and pre-planning for our annual conferences. We cover news in the ethnic areas, plus a column on ethnic resources."

For contributors, the editor writes, "We welcome articles that are meaningful and helpful toward building coalitions of ethnic groups that give us the TRUTH about ethnic groups, including not only similarities, but differences."

Ethnic Studies
ETHNIC FORUM
Editor: Lubomyr R. Wynar
Center for Study of Ethnic Publications
School of Library Science; Kent State Univ.
Kent, Ohio 44242
(216) 672-2784
Pub.: See description
Established 1979-1980
Sub.: U.S.:$20; International:$22.50
Distr.: Irregular-2 issues/year
Cir.: U.S.:400; Intl.:100
English text
0% non-English
Freelance articles accepted

SASE: Required
English ms.preference
Query recommended
Ms.length.: 20 pages
Payment: Not indic.
No photos,charts,etc.
Journal
Size: Not listed
Black/white
Regular paper
White color paper
No advertising
Deadline: Unknown
Outside group readers
No "kill" fee

The *Ethnic Forum* offers scholars, educators, librarians, media specialists, archivists, and students of ethnic issues a responsive forum for the analysis and discussion of all aspects of ethnicity and ethnic bibliography. This periodical is published by the Center for the Study of Ethnic Publications, Kent State University and Intercollegiate Academic Council on Ethnic Studies which serves Ohio.

Other articles published in the *Ethnic Forum* include critical reviews of books, reference sources and audiovisual materials in areas directly related to ethnic studies.

Prospective contributors should request a copy of "*Notes for Contributors*" before submitting manuscripts. The "*Notes*" are designed to help writers deal with manuscript specifications. (Author's note: Don't forget to enclose an SASE with your request for the "*Notes*.")

Ethnic Studies
EXPLORATIONS IN ETHNIC STUDIES
Editor: Gretchen Bataille
Department of English
Arizona State University
Tempe, Arizona 85287
(602) 965-3168
Pub.: Natl.Assn.for Ethnic Studies,Inc.
Established 1978
Sub.: U.S.:$25 +$5 Canada/Mexico;Others:+$10
Distribution: 5 times/year
Circulation: U.S.:250; Intl.:25
English text
0% non-English
Freelance articles accepted

SASE: Required
English ms.prefer
Query unnecessary
No ms.lgth.indicated
No pay; copy given
No photos
Magazine
Size: 5" x 8"
Black/white
Regular paper
White color paper
Display ads
Deadline varies
Some 100 libs.sub.
No "kill" fee

Explorations in Ethnic Studies is an interdisciplinary journal, published by the National Association for Ethnic Studies, Inc., (NAES), and is devoted to the study of ethnicity, ethnic groups, intergroup relations, and the cultural life of ethnic minorities. This periodical is published for professionals who are interested in the issues of ethnicity. Subscribers include scholars in many disciplines, student service personnel and students.

A subscription to *Explorations in Ethnic Studies* includes other publications. One journal supplement, *Explorations in Sights and Sounds*, is published once a year, and contains reviews of books and non-print media of interest to teachers, students, scholars in ethnic studies and community organizations.

The NAES also publishes *The Ethnic Reporter*. It is published twice a year and contains reports of the activities of the National Association for Ethnic Studies, Inc., such as conference and research opportunity news and some short articles.

Contributors interested in sending manuscripts to this journal should review the periodical and be familiar with the content material and style. This journal is available in approximately 100 libraries in the United States.

Subscriptions should be directed to: Ethnic Studies Institute; University of Nebraska; Lincoln, Nebraska. 68588-0335.

Ethnic Studies
NEW YORK AMSTERDAM NEWS
Editor: William K. Egyir
2340 Frederick Douglass Blvd.
New York
New York 10027
(212) 678-6600
Publisher: Wilbert A. Tatum
Established 1909
Subscription: Cost not indicated
Distribution: Weekly
Circulation: U.S.:48,000
English text
0% non-English
Freelance articles accepted

SASE: Not indicated
English ms. prefer
Query, letter
No ms.lgth.indicated
Payment/flat fee
Photos/credits/pay
Newspaper/Tabloid
Size: Not listed
Black/white
Paper type: Not listed
White color paper
Display, classified
Deadline: Monday
Corps, city politicians
No "kill" fee

New York Amsterdam News is a minority (group) oriented publication. It is described by the editor as "an advocate for justice, freedom, fair play and advancement of all people. Equal Opportunity for all races under the sun."

Ethnic Studies
PA.ETHNIC HERITAGE STUDIES
Editor: Joseph T. Makarewicz
4 G 31 Forbes Quadrangle
Pittsburgh
Pennsylvania 15260
(412) 648-7420
Publisher: PA Ethnic Heritage
Established 1975
Subscription: U.S.:$2; Intl.:$3
Distribution: Quarterly
Circulation: U.S.:2,250; Intl:50
English text
0% non-English
Freelance articles accepted

SASE: Not required
English manuscript prefer
Query, phone/letter o.k.
Ms.lgth.: 2,000-2,500 wds.
No pay for freelance
Photos accepted/credits
Magazine format
Size: Not listed
Black/white print
Newsprint paper
White color paper
No ads accepted
Deadline: None listed
Univ.,community libraries
No "kill" fee

The editor describes *Pennsylvania Ethnic Studies Newsletter* as a periodical which attempts to promote understanding of ethnic cultures and recognition of cross-cultural heritage. The ethnic interests of the periodical are described as general.

The editor's tips to contributors: "Manuscripts must be between 2,000 and 2,500 words, and for long articles and short news stories, any length is acceptable."

Ethnic Studies,Asian-Am.,Black,Hispanic,Nat.Am.	SASE: Required
EQUAL OPPORTUNITY MAGAZINE	Eng.ms.prefer
Editor: James Schneider	Query, letter
44 Broadway	No ms.lgth.listed
Greenlawn	Pay by word
New York 11740	Photos/credits/pay
(516) 261-8917	Magazine
Pub.: Equal Opportunity Pub.,Inc.	Size: 8" x 10"
Established 1969	B/white/color
Subscription: U.S.:$13/year	Glossy paper
Distribution: Three times/year	White paper
Circulation: U.S.:15,000 (controlled)	Display, classified
English text	Deadline: 6 bef.pub.
0% non-English	Coll.administrators
Freelance articles accepted	"Kill" fee: Unknown

The editor says about *Equal Opportunity Magazine*: "Our magazine is received by college students and young professionals who are Black, Hispanic, Native American and Asian-American. The focus is on career-guidance and job information."

This magazine provides role model profiles, career guidance topics and news of career opportunities for minorities.

The editors encourage writers to target articles specifically for the audience just described. Writers should present well-written, clean and professional manuscripts. Please include cover letter which details writing experience.

Those who wish to place either display or classified ads must submit the ad materials six weeks prior to desired publication date.

(Cross-referenced: Asian-American, Ethnic studies, Hispanic, Native American.)

F

Filipino
PHILIPPINE PRESS USA, THE
Editor: Agaton F. Cruz
943 Sierra Madre Dr.
Salinas
California 94102
(408) 424-3669
Publisher: Agaton F. Cruz
Established 1930
Subscription: U.S.$7
Distribution: Monthly
Circulation: U.S.:5,000
English text
0% non-English
Freelance: No information
SASE: No information
English ms.preference
Query: No information
No ms.length indicated
Payment: No information
Photos
Newspaper
Size: 14" x 23"
Black/white
Newsprint paper
White color paper
Display, classified
Deadline: Not indicated
Outside readers: Unknown
"Kill" fee: No information

The Philippine Press USA contains special columns by writers, editorial/commentary, social, club, fraternal, organization news, cultural and governmental information of interest to the Filipino population. This newspaper has bureau contacts in San Francisco, Milpitas and San Bruno, California, and Quezon City, Philippines.

The editor provided no specific tips for contributors, but if a writer has articles which may be of interest, write to the editor first.

Filipino
PHILIPPINE REPORT
Editor: Joel Rocamora
P.O. Box 40090
Berkeley
California 94704
(415) 548-2546
Publisher: Philippine Resource Center
Established October 1984
Subscription: U.S.:$15; Intl.:$25
Distribution: Monthly
Circulation: U.S.:1,700; Intl.:300
English text
0% non-English
Freelance articles accepted
SASE: No response
English ms.preference
Query, letter
No ms.length indicated
No payment
Photo/credits/pay
Format: No response
Size: 8.5" x 11"
Black/white
Newsprint paper
White color paper
No ads
Deadline: Not indicated
Various outside groups
No "kill" fee

Philippine Report publishes information on the issues and events in the Philippines, and the activities of Filipino groups in North America.

Among the *Phillipine Report's* non-ethnic interest readers, the editor lists individuals and institutions interested in the Philippines such as peace groups, women's groups, peasant groups, student groups, and so forth.

This publication supports the struggle of the Filipino people for peace, justice and genuine sovereignty.

The editor did not provide any specific tips for contributors.

Filipino-American
FILIPINO-AMERICAN HERALD
Editor: Sluggo Rigor
2824 S. Brandon
Seattle
Washington 98108
(206) 725-6606
Publisher: E.A. Francisco
Established 1940
Subscription: U.S.:$8
Distribution: Monthly
Sub.: U.S.:8,000 (Also controlled)
Tagalog, English text
10% non-English (Tagalog)
Freelance articles accepted

SASE: Not indicated
English ms.preference
Query, letter
No ms.length indicated
No payment
Photos/credits/pay
Newspaper/tabloid
Size: 10" x 17"
Black/white, some color
Paper type: Unknown
White color paper
Display, classified
Deadline: 5th each month
Outside group readers
No "kill" fee

Filipino-American Herald is, according to the editor, "very much concerned with community news, with good coverage of state and national news." The editor writes that the paper gives praise when appropriate and criticism to those on the negative side (of the issues).

Finnish
AMERIKAN UUTISET
Editor: Aarne A. Aaltonen
444 W. Lantana Road
Lantana
Florida 33462
(305) 588-9770
Publisher: Amerikan Uutiset
Established 1932
Subscription: Cost not listed
Distribution: Weekly
Cir.: U.S.:1,800; Intl.:100-200
Finnish, English text
80% non-English
Freelance acceptance: No response

SASE: No response
Ms.lang.: No preference
Query: No response
No ms.length indicated
No payment
Photos/credits/no pay
Tabloid
Size: 10" x 16"
Black/white/color
Newsprint paper
White color paper
Display, classified
Deadline: 1 wk.in advance
Outside readers: Unknown
No "kill" fee

American Uutiset publishes information to help preserve the Finnish traditions, heritage and language in the U.S.A. The tabloid is further described as building a contact between ethnic areas in the U.S. and allows Finnish-speaking Americans to express themselves in their inherited language.

Amerikan Uutiset publishes news from Finland and the world in Finnish.

Contributors are advised that anything connected with the Finnish community in the U.S.A. is welcome, including short stories, reports and news.

Finnish-American
FINN-AM NEWSLETTER
Editor: Gene A. Knapp
P.O. Box 5522
Portland
Oregon 97208
(503) 654-0448
Pub.: Finnish-Amer.Hist.Soc.West
Established 1974
Subscription: U.S.:$5; Intl.:$5
Distribution: Quarterly
Circulation: U.S.:326; Intl.:3
Finnish, English text
l0% or less non-English
Freelance articles accepted

SASE: Not required
English ms.preference
Query unnecessary
No ms.length indicated
No payment
Photos accepted/credits
Newsletter
Size: 8.5" x 11"
Black/white
Regular bond paper
White color paper
No advertising
Deadline: Not indicated
No outside group readers
No "kill" fee

Finn-Am Newsletter publishes information about the Finnish-American involvement in the history of the United States. "The readers are supportive of, or interested in, our publication of Finnish-American monographs," according to the editor.

The editorial content of the *Finn-Am Newsletter* is described as containing society news and items of interest to Finnish-American history buffs. The editor writes, "The content is aimed at enhancing interest in and knowledge of Finnish-Americana, especially in the West."

For contributors, the editor writes, "Specific coverage of people, places, things and events of historical importance to Finn-Amer. people (is preferred).

"This is a non-profit, volunteer-oriented society. Writing is rated as amateur, and all contributions are subject to free editing in such a manner as to align the work offered to a rough conformation to our editorial style.

"Our newsletter supports a larger commitment to special publications of twenty-five to one hundred pages in monograph form."

Finnish-American	SASE: Not required
FINNAM NEWS	English ms.preference
Editor: Gene A. Knapp	Query, letter
P.O.Box 5522	No ms.length indicated
Portland	No payment
Oregon 97208	Photos/credits/no pay
(503) 654-0448	Newspaper
Pub.: Finnish-Amer.Hist.Soc.of West	Size: 8.5" x 11"; 6pg.
Established 1965	Black/white
Sub.: U.S.Membership dues:$5/yr.	Paper type: 60 lb.
Distribution: Quarterly	White color paper
Circulation: U.S.:356; Intl.:4	No advertising
English, some Finnish text	Deadline: Not indicated
Negligible % non-English	Libs.,colleges, univ.
Freelance articles accepted	"Kill" fee:N/A

Finnam News publishes articles exclusively about Finnish-American and Finnish history in the Western United States with on-going research as a focus, although not in genealogy. The editor writes that the publication has twenty l00-page illustrated special publications which are free to annual members. A current listing of special publications is available from the publication office.

Special publications can be purchased individually or in complete sets. (Author's note: Suggest enclosing an SASE when requesting list of publications.)

For contributors, the editor writes, "Amateur status is preserved in staff publication contributions through the by-laws of our non-profit society. Editing is provided; expert writing is not required. Historical facts, correctness and the impact of subject matter are judgement criteria."

Finnish-American
NEW YORKIN UUTISET
Editor: Anita Rothovius
4422-8th Ave.
Brooklyn
New York 11220
No telephone listing
Pub.: The Finnish Newspaper Co.,Inc.
Established Fall 1906
Sub.: U.S.:$25/yr; Intl.:$30/yr
Distribution: Weekly
Cir.: U.S.:2,000;Intl.:500
Finnish, English text
60% non-English
Freelance articles accepted

SASE: Not indicated
No ms.lang.preference
Query, letter
No ms.length indicated
Payment: Ask editor
Photos: No response
Tabloid
Size: Not listed
Black/white
Paper type: No response
White color paper
Display, classified
Deadline: Friday ea.wk.
Outside readers: Unknown
"Kill" fee: No response

New Yorkin Uutiset publishes articles of Finnish-American human interests, cultural information, and heritage matters that relate to Finland and the United States.

The editor suggests that contributors call and check to find out what is needed before sending manuscripts.

Franco-American
BULLETIN DE LA FEDERATION FEMININE
Editor: Marthe Biron Peloguin
1 Leland Road
Westford
Massachusetts 01886
(617) 692-6370
Pub.: La Fed.Feminine-Franco Americaine
Established 1952
Subscription: U.S.:$3; Intl.:$4
Distribution: Quarterly
Circulation: U.S:Total 500
French text
100% non-English
Freelance articles accepted

SASE: Required
French ms.preferred
Query, letter
No ms.lgth.indicated
No payment
Photos/credits
Format: Not indicated
Size: Not listed
Black/white
Glossy paper
White color paper
Ad use: Not indicated
Deadline: Unknown
Outside group readers
No "kill" fee

Bulletin De La Federation Franco-Americaine Feminine is described as publishing an overview of information about Franco-American cultural activities in New England, promotion of the deeper knowledge of the French civilization and its contribution to the building of North America.

The editor of *Bulletin De La Federation Franco-Americaine Feminine* writes, "It (the publication) focuses on the need to explore your (French) roots, develop a strong cultural identity and explore all the means of utilizing our inherited French culture to serve our country and foster better international communication."

G

German
AMERIKA WOCHE (AMERICA WEEK)
Editor: Werner V. Baroni
4732 No. Lincoln Ave.
Chicago
Illinois 60625
(312) 275-5054
Publishers: E. & W. Baroni
Established 1972
Subscription: U.S.:$27.50
Distribution: Weekly
Circulation: U.S.:25,000
German text
90% non-English
Freelance articles accepted

SASE: No response
German manuscript prefer
Query: No response
No ms.length indicated
Pay for freelance
Photos/pay
Newspaper
Size: Not listed
Black/white/color
Newsprint paper
White color paper
Display, classified
Deadline: Every Monday
Outside group readers
No "kill" fee

The editor of *Amerika Woche (America Week)* provided no additional information.

Payment for freelance articles is per line.

German
CALIFORNIA STAATS-ZEITUNG
Editor: Peter Teichmann
P.O. Box 26308
1201 N. Alvarado
Los Angeles, California 90026
(213) 413-5500
Publisher: Peter Teichmann
Established 1890
Subscription: Fee not listed
Distribution: Weekly
Circulation: U.S.:14,000
German text
% non-English not listed
No freelance/Staff assigned

SASE: No response
German ms.preference
Query: Not specified
No ms.length indicated
No payment
Photos: No response
Newspaper
Size: Not listed
Black/white
Paper type: Not listed
Color paper: Not listed
Display, classified
Deadline: Tuesday A.M.
Colleges,univ.,newsstands
"Kill" fee: No response

California Staats-Zeitung is a German language newspaper. No other information concerning the contents of this periodical was provided.

German-Jewish
AUFBAU
Editors: Gert Niers & Henry Marx
2121 Broadway
New York
New York 10023
(212) 873-7400
Publisher: New World Club
Established 1934
Subscription: U.S.:$41; Intl.:$63
Distribution: Biweekly
Cir.: U.S.:22,000; Intl.:8,000
German text
99% non-English
Freelance articles accepted

SASE: Required
German ms.preference
Query, letter
No ms.length indicated
Pay/flat fee
Photos/credits/pay
Tabloid
Size: Not listed
Black/white/color
Newsprint paper
White color paper
Display, classified
Deadline: Fri.before pub.
Foreign govts.,ed.instit.
No "kill" fee

Aufbau publishes political and cultural information. If manuscripts are unsolicited, they must be in GERMAN only. No responsibility is assumed for manuscripts sent to the editors.

Germans from Pommern
DIE POMMERSCHEN LEUTE
Editor: Myron E. Gruenwald
1260 Westhaven Dr.
Oshkosh
Wisconsin 54904
(414) 235-7398
Publisher: Myron E. Gruenwald
Established June 1982
Subscription: U.S.:$10; Intl.:$12
Distribution: Monthly
Circulation: U.S.:719; Intl.:15
English, German text
2-3% non-English
No freelance articles/Staff assigned

SASE: No response
English ms.preference
Query, letter
No ms.length indicated
No payment
No photos/credit
Newspaper
Size: 8.5" x 11"
Black/white
Regular paper
White color paper
Ads: None
Deadline: Not listed
No outside group readers
No "kill" fee

Die Pommerschen Leute focuses on the descendants of immigrants from the German Baltic Duchy of Pommern, with emphasis on genealogical, historical and cultural information.

This periodical is described as interpreting American life in terms of history and values of Northern German immigrants and develops pride, along with knowledge, of cultural inheritance.

The editor's tips for contributors: "Would prefer a personal experience as a member of our ethnic group."

Germans from Russia
AMER.HIST.SOC.GERMANS FROM RUSSIA,JOUR.OF
Editor: Ruth M. Amen
631 "D" Street
Lincoln
Nebraska 68502
(402) 474-3363
Publisher: Am.Hist.Soc.Ger.from Russia
Established 1970
Subscription: Members only; no subs.
Distribution: Quarterly
Circulation: U.S.:6,000;Intl.:500
English text
0% non-English
Freelance articles accepted

SASE: Required
Engl.ms.prefer
Query, letter
No ms.lgth.indic.
No payment
Photos/credits
Magazine
Size: 8.5" x 11"
Black/white
Regular paper
White color paper
No ads
Deadline: Unk.
No outside rdrs.
No "kill" fee

The *Journal of the American Historical Society of Germans from Russia* publishes information as it relates to the history and culture of Germans from Russia.

The editor's tips to contributors: "All articles must relate to Germans from Russia--history, culture, folklore and genealogy."

Germans of Russian Descent
HERITAGE REVIEW
Editor: Armand Bauer
1008 E. Central Ave.
Bismarck
North Dakota 58501
(701) 223-7061
Pub.: Germans fm.Russia Heritage Soc.
Established 1971
Subscription: U.S.:$20; Intl.:$20
Distribution: Quarterly
Circulation: U.S.:1,797; Intl.:203
English text
0% non-English
Freelance articles accepted

SASE: No response
English ms.preference
Query: No response
No ms.length indicated
No payment
Photos/no pay
Magazine/journal
Size: 8.5" x 11"
Black/white
Regular paper
White paper;color cover
No advertising
Deadline: Not listed
Some outside group rdrs.
No "kill" fee paid

Heritage Review publishes articles about genealogy and the cultural history of the Germans from Russia, and will accept freelance articles about the ethnic heritage of the group. The organization, Germans from Russia Heritage Society has a bookstore located at 1008 East Central Avenue, Bismarck, North Dakota, 58501. The store is open from 10 a.m. to 4 p.m., Monday through Friday and accepts mail orders for their various publications.

The book list from the Society's store is extensive, and includes subjects that cover a variety of topics of interest to the group. Albums, cassettes, eight tracks, slides and tapes, maps, note pads, and many other items are available for sale through the bookstore and by mail order.

Greek
HELLENIC DIASPORA, JOURNAL OF THE
Editor: Yiorgos Chouliaras
337 West 36th St.
New York
New York 10018
(212) 279-9586
Publisher: Pella Publishing Co.
Established 1974
Subscription: U.S.:$15; Intl.:$20
Distribution: Quarterly
Circulation: U.S.:500; Intl.:200
Greek, English text
10% non-English
Freelance articles accepted

SASE: Required
English ms.preference
Query ltr.ONLY;3 mo.resp.
Ms.lgth max.: 20,000 words
No payment
No photos printed
Magazine
Size: 5.5" x 8.5"
Black/white print
Newsprint paper
White color paper
No ad information
Deadline: Not listed
No outside group readers
No "kill" fee

Journal of the Hellenic Diaspora readers' interests are described by the editors as "anything having to do with modern Greek history, politics, literature and culture." The editors also write that the magazine publishes articles concerned with the entire spectrum of scholarly, critical and artistic work based on contemporary Greece.

The editors ask that articles be original and not published previously.

A query letter is necessary for the editors to review the nature of the article to be submitted. Editors say they have a backlog of correspondence which means prospective contributors may have to wait about three months for a response.

Freelance articles must be no longer than 20,000 words, double-spaced, and, if author wishes to have manuscript returned, an (self-addressed, stamped envelope) SASE is a must.

The Journal does not publish novels, fiction or poetry.

Greek, Greek-American
HELLENIC JOURNAL,THE
Executive editor: Tim Kaun
527 Commercial Street
San Francisco
California 94111
negotiated (415) 781-3684
Publisher: Frank P. Agnost
Established April 10, 1975
Sub.: U.S.:$15/yr.; Intl.:$25/yr.
Distribution: Biweekly
Circulation: 3,000 total
Greek, English text
15% non-English
Freelance articles accepted

SASE: Required
English ms.preference
Query, letter
No ms.length indicated
Pay negotiated
Photos/credits/pay
Tabloid
Size: 11.5" x 17.5"
Black/white/color
Newsprint paper
White color paper
Display ads
Deadline: Fri.bef.pub.
Philhellenes,institutions
"Kill" fee: No response

The Hellenic Journal publishes news of Greece and the Greek-American community. Content ranges from political and social to cultural information.

The editor gave no suggestions for contributors.

Greek, Greek-American, Cypriot
AHEPAN
Editor: Elias Valanton
1707 L St., N.W.; Suite 200
Washington
D.C. 20036
(202) 628-4974
Publisher: Ahepan
Established 1928
Sub.: U.S.:$10 (Controlled)
Distribution: Quarterly
Cir.: U.S.:35,000; Intl.:2,000
English text
5% non-English (less than)
Freelance articles accepted

SASE: Not required
English ms.preference
Query unnecessary
No ms.length indicated
Pay/flat fee
Photos: Staff assigned
Magazine
Size: Not listed
Black/white/color
Glossy paper
Color paper not listed
Display
Deadline: Not listed
No outside group readers
No "kill" fee

Ahepan publishes fraternal information and articles about Greece, Cyprus and Greek-American issues.

The editor had no suggestions for contributors.

(Cross-referenced: Cypriot.)

H

Hispanic
CAMINOS MAGAZINE
Editor: R. Rodriguez
Box 54307
Los Angeles, California 90054

The questionnaire was unclaimed. No forwarding address available.

Hispanic
EL HISPANO NEWS
Editor: A.B. Collado
900 Park Ave. S.W.
Albuquerque
New Mexico 87102
(505) 243-6161
Publisher: A.B. Collado
Established June 17,1966
Sub.: U.S.:$8/yr;$9/yr.outside New Mexico
Distribution: Weekly
Circulation: U.S.:11,990; Intl.:10
100% Spanish text
100% non-English
Freelance articles accepted

SASE: No response
No ms.lang.preference
Query unnecessary
No ms.length indicated
Pays by news story
Photos/credits/pay
Newspaper
Size: 5" x 14"
Black/white/color
Newsprint paper
White color paper
Display, classified
Deadline: Tuesday
Non-Hispanic rdrs.:15%
Pays "kill" fee by pages

El Hispano News is an independent pro-Hispanic newspaper, and the editor describes the ethnic interest of the readers as those who "keep the Spanish language alive in the bilingual state of New Mexico."

The editor provided no tips for contributors, but prospective contributors might benefit by reviewing a copy of the publication prior to submitting manuscripts.

Hispanic
EL NOTICIARIO
Managing Editor: Debra Schiebeel
20 F St. N.W.; Second Floor
Washington
D.C. 20001
(202) 628-9600
Pub.: National Council of La Raza
Established 1979
Subscription: Controlled (Free)
Distribution: Quarterly
Circulation: U.S.:4,500
English text
0% non-English
No freelance articles accepted

SASE: Not applicable
English ms.preference
Query: Not applicable
Ms.length: Not applicable
Pay: Not applicable
Photos: Staff assigned
Newsletter
Size: 8.5" x 11" (6 pages)
Black/white
Glossy paper
White color paper
No advertising
Deadline: Not applicable
Corp.,foundations, others
"Kill" fee: Not applicable

El Noticiario publicizes the activities of the National Council of La Raza and its network of affiliated communities.

The editorial content is focused on activities and accomplishments of the National Council of La Raza and its local affiliates, Hispanic community-based organizations. The Council serves and represents all Hispanic subgroups in the United States.

El Noticiario contains articles about Hispanic and non-Hispanic policy makers, institutions, the mainstream press and the general public. The editor cites corporations, foundations, non-profit groups, public officials, institutions and media as the non-ethnic readers who receive the publication.

The periodical publishes an analysis of public policy issues of special concern to Hispanics: for example, education, employment, immigration, civil rights enforcement, language issues, housing and community development, as well as the Hispanic elderly. The categories mentioned are not a complete list of all possible areas of interest.

This publication is an "in-house" newsletter.

Hispanic
HISPANIC MONITOR/EL OBSERVADOR
Old Address
250 W.57th St.; Room 232
New York, New York 10107

The survey questionnaire unclaimed and no forwarding address was available.

Hispanic
LA RED/THE NET HOTLINE
Editor: Dr.Arturo Madrid
16161 Ventura Blvd.; Suite 830
Encino, California 91436-2504
Pub.: Roberto Cabello-Argandona

Refer to *Lector, The Hispanic Book Review Journal*, for information concerning *La Red/The Net Hotline.*

Hispanic
LECTOR, The Hispanic Book Review Jour.
Editor: Roberto Cabello Argandona
16161 Ventura Blvd.; Suite 830
Encino
California 91436
(818) 990-1885
Publisher: Floricanto Press
Established 1982
Subscription: U.S.:$45; Intl.: $50
Distribution: Biannual
Circulation: U.S. and Intl.:3,000
Spanish, English text
10% non-English
Freelance articles accepted

SASE: Required
English ms.preference
Query, letter
No ms.lgth.indicated
Payment/flat fee
Photos/credits/pay
Magazine
Size: 8.5" x 11"
Black/white, color cover
Glossy cover; 50lb.paper
White color paper
Display, classified
Deadline:15th April; Aug.
Public, academic libs.
"Kill" fee flat rate

Lector, The Hispanic Book Review Journal, reviews books written in English, Spanish or bilingual, published in the United States, Spain, and Latin America of interest to the Hispanic community.

The editorial content is described as "independent book review and articles on literature, writers and publishing trends."

Floricanto Press also publishes *La Red/The Net Hotline: The Hispanic Journal of Education, Commentary, and Reviews*, a periodical which contains announcements, employment opportunities, news about events, grants and fellowships. Additionally, papers on research, development and issues in education are reviewed for possible publication.

Subscription rates are divided into categories for institutions, individuals and students.

In the sample copy, the editor of *LaRed/The Net*, writes, "We will respond to submissions in a timely fashion. Request guidelines for submitting articles, reports and commentaries."

The editor's tips to contributors: "Write articles in plain language, omit jargon and professional buzzwords. We are interested in Hispanic and Latin American writers."

Hispanic, Asian
EASTSIDE SUN
Editor: John Sanchez
2912 E. Brooklyn Ave.
Los Angeles
California 90033
(213) 263-5743
Publisher: Delores Sanchez
Established 1945
Sub.: U.S.:$29.50;Intl.:$29.50+postage
Distribution: Weekly
Circulation: Total:13,600
English, Spanish text
30% Spanish; 70% English
Freelance articles accepted

SASE: No response
No ms.lang.preference
Query: No response
Ms.lgth.: 2 pages or less
No pay for freelance
Photos/credits/no pay
Newspaper
Size: 13" x 21"
Black/white/color
Newsprint paper
White color paper
Display, classified
Deadline: Fri.b.pub.week
Corp., govt.leaders,others
No "kill" fee

Eastside Sun publishes information on local or national news of interest to the Hispanic community. According to the editor, some Asian readers also receive *Eastside Sun*, so editors include some Asian news. The newspaper is described as "very democratic."

The editor asks that contributors limit submissions to two pages or shorter as space is at a premium.

(Cross-referenced: Asian.)

Hispanic, Black
AIM MAGAZINE
Editor: Ruth Apilado
7308 So. Eberhart
Chicago
Illinois 60619
(312) 874-6184
Publisher: Ruth Apilado
Established January 1974
Subscription: U.S.:$8;Intl.:$10
Distribution: Quarterly
Cir.: U.S.:8,000; 4,000 controlled
English text
0% non-English
Freelance articles accepted

SASE: No response
English ms.preference
Query unnecessary
Ms.length: Not listed
Payment
Photo/credits/no pay
Magazine
Size: 11.5" x 8"
Black/white
Newsprint paper
White color paper
Display
Deadline: 15th M.,Je.,S.,Dec.
Colleges,univ.,gen.public
No "kill" fee

The editor of *Aim Magazine* states the ethnic-interest of the periodical as follows:

"We're interested in promoting racial harmony and peace--in correcting false racial opinions of the majority--building confidence and pride in black and Hispanic Americans--all through the written word."

These ideals are reflected in the description of the objectives of *Aim Magazine* by the editor who writes, "Often we select an unknown in a community and profile him/her, who is making a contribution to social progress."

With respect to tips to contributors, the editor suggests that writers look for an event that has made a great contribution toward solving racial problems.

(Cross-referenced: Black.)

Hispanic,Asian-Am.;Blk.,Ethnic Studies,Nat.Am.	SASE: Required
EQUAL OPPORTUNITY MAGAZINE	Engl.ms.prefer
Editor: James Schneider	Query, letter
44 Broadway	No ms.lgth.listed
Greenlawn	Pay by word
New York 11740	Photos/credits/pay
(516) 261-8917	Magazine
Pub.: Equal Opportunity Pub.,Inc.	Size: 8" x 10"
Established 1969	Black/white/color
Subscription: U.S.:$13/yr.	Glossy paper
Distribution: Three times/year	White paper
Circulation: U.S.:15,000 (controlled)	Display, classified
English text	Deadline:6 wk.b.pub.
0% non-English	College adm.
Freelance articles accepted	"Kill" fee: Unknown

The editor says about *Equal Opportunity Magazine*: "Our magazine is received by college students and young professionals who are Black, Hispanic, Native American and Asian-American. The focus is on career guidance and job information."

This magazine provides role model profiles, career-guidance topics and news of career opportunities for minorities.

The editors encourage writers to target articles specifically for the audience just described. Writers should present well-written, clean and professional manuscripts. Please include cover letter which details writing experience.

Those who wish to place either display or classified ads must submit the ad materials six weeks prior to desired publication date.

(Cross-referenced: Hispanic, Asian-American, Black, Ethnic studies, Native American.)

Hispanic-Mexican
EL CHICANO COMMUNITY NEWSPAPER
Editor: Gloria Macias
P.O.Box 827
Colton
California 92324
(714) 825-1145
Publisher: Gloria Macias
Established 1969
Subscription: Fee not listed
Distribution: Weekly
Circulation: No information
Spanish, English text
10% non-English
Freelance articles accepted

SASE: Required
No ms.lang.preference
Query unnecessary
No ms.length indicated
Pay/column inch
Photos/credits
Newspaper
Size: Broadsheet
Print process: Unknown
Newsprint paper
Paper color: Not listed
Display, classified
Deadline: Monday ea.week
Some outside gp.readers
No "kill" fee

El Chicano Community Newspaper has an Hispanic focus with an emphasis on Mexican-Americans in the southwestern United States. Local news coverage is included with some national Hispanic news.

The editor provided no tips for contributors.

Hispanics in Michigan
EL RENACIMIENTO
Editor: Jose A. Lopez
1132 N. Washington
Lansing
Michigan 48906
(517) 485-4389
Publisher: Jose A. Lopez
Established 1970
Subscription: No information
Distribution: Monthly
Circulation: U.S.: I0,000 controlled
Spanish, English text
40% non-English
Freelance articles accepted

SASE: Required
No ms.lang.preferred
Query unnecessary
No ms.length indicated
No pay
Photos/credits
Tabloid
Size: Not listed
Black/white/color
Newsprint paper
White color paper
Display, classified
Deadline: 15th of month
Coll., univ.libraries
No "kill" fee

El Renacimiento is written for Michigan's Hispanic population, of which the largest percentage are Mexican-American, mostly third generation Hispanics who have pride in their culture, according to the editor. The editor describes the content of the periodical as "middle of the road" and educational.

No tips for contributors were provided. As with most periodicals, it is useful to review the periodical under consideration prior to sending either a query or a manuscript to the editor of the publication.

Hungarian
CALIFORNIAI MAGYARSAG(CA Hungarians)
Editor: Maria Fenyes
207 S. Western Ave; No.201
Los Angeles
California 90004
(213) 463-3473
Publisher: Maria Fenyes
Established October 6, 1922
Subscription: U.S.:$21; Intl.:$25
Distribution: Weekly
Circulation: U.S.:6,750; Intl.:750
English, Hungarian text
% non-English: Minimal; some ads
Freelance articles accepted

SASE: No response
English ms. preferred
Query: No response
No ms.length indicated
Payment, flat fee
Photos accepted
Tabloid
Size: 17" x 11";12-24pp.
Black/white (offset)
Paper type: Unknown
White color paper
Display, classified
Deadline: Monday
No outside group readers
"Kill" fee: No response

Californiai Magyarsag publishes information about American and East European domestic and foreign politics and cultural events.

Non-English language published is, according to the editor, limited to some advertisements.

The editor provided no suggestions for contributors.

Hungarian
HUNGARIAN WORD (AMERIKAI MAGYAR SZO)
Editor: Zoltan Deak
130 E. 16th St.
New York
New York 10003
(212) 254-0397
Publisher: Hungarian Word, Inc.
Established 1953
Sub.: U.S.:$20/yr.; Intl.:$25/yr.
Distribution: Weekly
Circulation: U.S.:1,700;Intl.:300
Hungarian, one page English text
%non-English not specified
Freelance accepted: No response

SASE: No response
No ms.lang.listed
Query: No response
Ms.lgth.not indicated
Payment: Not specified
Photos: Not specified
Format: Not specified
Size: Not listed
Black/white
Newsprint paper
White color paper
Classified
Deadline: Thursday
Outside group readers
"Kill" fee: Not indic.

Hungarian Word (Amerikai Magyar Szo) ethnic-interests are described as general. The newspaper publishes one page in English and the remainder in Hungarian. No information was provided on the number of pages in the newspaper.

Hungarian
SZIVARVANY
Editor: Ferenc Mozsi
561 W. Diversey Parkway
Chicago
Illinois 60614
(312) 477-1485
Publisher: Framo Publishing
Established 1980
Sub.: U.S.:$25;Intl.:$25/+$9 Air Mail
Distribution: Weekly
Circulation: U.S.:600; International:400
Hungarian text
l00% non-English
No freelance articles accepted

SASE: Not required
Hungarian ms.preferred
Query: Not needed
No ms.length indicated
No payment
No photos/cr./no pay
Magazine
Size: 5.5" x 8.5"
Black/white
Newsprint paper
White color paper
No ads
Deadline: Not indicated
No outside group readers
No "kill" fee

Szivarvany focuses on Hungarian literature in the USA, abroad and in Hungary, such as essays, poetry, short stories, a critic's section, artistic illustrations, translations or reflections on contemporary works.

The editor describes the editorial content as "publishing information on good works and well-done scripts."

With respect to suggestions for contributors, the editor writes, "Try to be more up-to-date, even outside of the native country."

I

Indian
INDIA WEST
Editor: Bina Murarka
5901 Christie Ave.
Emeryville
California 94608
(415) 652-0265
Publisher: Ramesh Murarka
Established 1975
Sub.: U.S.:$22; Intl.:$22+postage
Distribution: Weekly
Circulation: U.S.:10,000; Intl.:50
English text
0% non-English
Freelance articles accepted

SASE: Required
English ms.preference
Query, letter
No ms.lgth.indicated
Pay based on story idea
Photos/credits/payment
Tabloid
Size: 11.5" x 17"
Black/white/color
Newsprint paper
White color paper
Display, classified
Deadline: Every Monday
Libs., other readers
"Kill" fee paid

India West is written for people from India who are interested in India and the subcontinent. Readers from outside the group are described as people with similar interests. Some libraries receive this periodical.

The editorial content of India West is described as containing news from India and about the Indian community in the United States. Examples of the articles include feature stories, news, profiles, business, entertainment, sports, book reviews, science notes and so forth. The focus is on the Indo-American community.

For contributors, the editor writes, "We do not really solicit articles, but ideas are welcome."

Indian
NEWS INDIA
Editor: John Perry
99 Lexington Avenue
New York
New York 10016
(212) 481-3110 or 481-3115
Publisher: John Perry
Established 1975
Sub.: U.S.:$20; Intl.:$75
Distribution: Weekly
Cir.: U.S.:17,800; Intl.:600
English text
0% non-English
Freelance articles accepted
SASE: Required
No ms.language preference
Query: No preference
No ms.length indicated
Pay/fl.fee/news article
Photo/credits/pay negotiated
Tabloid
Size: 17" x 12"
Black/white/color
Newsprint paper
White color paper
Display, classified
Deadline: Saturday, 6 p.m.
Libs.,univ.,social-cult.gps.
"Kill" fee paid

News India is described as a leader in promoting the 750,000 strong Indian community to have a permanent hold in the United States and promotes active participation in U.S. politics.

The editorial content is, according to the editor, "very pro-Indian and presently very critical of the ruling Congress party of Rajiv Gandhi, and supports stronger Indo-Jewish relations and Indo-Israeli ties."

The editor suggests that contributors check first regarding the subject of possible freelance articles.

With respect to other suggestions to contributors, the editor writes, "Don't write for money alone. Keep the 750,000 Indian community, settled in the USA, in mind (when writing)."

Irish
IRISH HERALD NEWSPAPER
Editor: John Whooley
2123 Market Street
San Francisco
California 94114
(415) 621-2200
Publisher: John Whooley
Established 1962
Subscription: U.S.:$12; International:$23
Distribution: Monthly
Cir.: U.S.:5,000;International:1,000
English text
0% non-English
Freelance articles accepted
SASE: Required
English ms.preference
Query, letter o.k.
No ms.length indicated
Payment: Editor's decision
Photos/credits/poss.pay
Tabloid
Size: Not listed
Black/white
Newsprint paper
White color paper
Display
Deadline: 20th prev.month
Libraries, cultural org.
No "kill" fee

Irish Herald Newspaper contains news from Ireland, local events, reviews of Irish books, record news, financial column and editorial comment.

Irish, Celtic, Scottish, Welsh
THE DRAGON, THE THISTLE, THE HARP
Editor: J.D. Holsinger
2214 E. Cherryvale
Springfield
Missouri 65804
No phone listing
Pub: Celtic Society of Missouri Ozarks
Established l987
Subscription: Fee not listed
Distribution: Quarterly
Circulation: U.S.:50
English text
%non-English: Minimal
Freelance accepted: Editor's decision

SASE: Not indicated
Ms.lang.: Not listed
Query, letter
No ms.length indicated
Pay policy: Not indic.
Photos: No response
Newsletter
Size: 8.5" x 11" - 8.5" x 16"
Black/white
Bond regular paper
White color paper
No ads accepted
Deadline: Not listed
No outside gp.readers
"Kill" fee: No response

The Dragon, The Thistle, The Harp is a publication which, according to the editor, "tries to have articles on the Welsh, Scottish, and Irish, especially in Missouri."

A sample copy of *The Dragon, The Thistle, The Harp* contained articles about significant events, origin of Celtic names in the Ozarks, pronunciation technique discussion and news about members.

The editor writes that the publication has no experience with people "sending articles."

(Cross-referenced: Celtic, Scottish, Welsh.)

Irish-American
IRISH ADVOCATE
Editor: James N. O'Connor
15 Park Row
New York
New York 10038
(212) 233-4672
Publisher: James N. O'Connor
Established 1893
Subscription: U.S.:$10; Intl.:$25
Distribution: Weekly
Circulation: U.S.:17,500; Intl.:Few
English text
0% non-English
Freelance articles accepted

SASE: Required
English ms.preference
Query, letter
Ms.lgth.not indicated
No payment
Photos/credits
Tabloid
Size: 11" x 15"
Black/white/color
Newsprint paper
White color paper
Display, classified
Deadline: Monday evening
Colleges,law schools,politicians
No "kill" fee

The *Irish Advocate* publishes articles focused on Irish-American non-political and non-sectarian interests. The contents of this periodical are also described by the editor as "liberal, progressive."

For contributors, the editor writes, "Make it short and to the point, and give details. Manuscripts should be typewritten, double-spaced, and on one side of paper."

Irish-American
IRISH ECHO
Editor: John Thornton
309 Fifth Ave.
New York
New York 10066
(212) 686-1266
Publisher: John Grimes
Established 1928
Subscription: U.S.:$18; Intl.:$40
Distribution: Weekly
Cir.: U.S.:38,000; Intl.:1,000
English text
0% non-English
Freelance articles accepted

SASE: Required
English manuscript prefer
Query, letter
No ms.length indicated
Pay: Seven cents/word
Photos: Staff assigned
Tabloid
Size: 10" x 14"
Black/white/color
Newsprint paper
White color paper
Display, classified
Deadline: Friday noon
No-outside group readers
"Kill" fee: No response

Irish Echo is described by the editor as written and published to appeal to the Irish-American community.

The editor did not list any other description nor provide any suggestions for contributors.

Italian; Italian-American
AIHA NEWSLETTER
Editor: Jerome Krase
209 Flagg Place
Staten Island
New York 10304
(718) 667-6628 or (718) 499-7117
Pub.: American Italian Historical Assn.
Established 1969
Subscription: U.S.:$25/year
Distribution: Quarterly
Circulation: U.S.:800; Intl.:200
Italian, English text
5% non-English
Freelance articles accepted

SASE: No response
No ms.lang.preference
Query, letter
No ms.length indicated
No payment
No photos accepted
Tabloid
Size: 8.5" x 11"
Black/white
Paper type: Bond
White color paper
Display
Deadline: Not listed
Academic orgs.,colleges
No "kill" fee

AIHA Newsletter is published by the American Italian Historical Association for Italian and Italian-Americans and Italians in other countries.

The editor suggests that contributors "read newsletter, attend conferences and join the AIHA."

Italian, Italian-American
ECHO
Managing Editor: Doreen A. Demitu
124 Webster Avenue
Providence
Rhode Island 02904
(401) 942-8900
Publisher: Richard P. Baccari
Established September 1897
Sub.: U.S.:$10; Intl.:$40
Distribution: Bimonthly
Cir.: U.S.:15,000; Intl.:50
English text
1% non-English
Freelance articles accepted

SASE: Required
English ms.preference
Query, letter
No ms.length indicated
Pay/fl.fee/story extent
Photos/cr./pay per assign
Tabloid
Size: 8.5" x 16"
Black/white/color
Newsprint paper
Buff paper color
Display, classified
Deadline: Mon.before pub.
Comm.groups,profs.,others
No "kill" fee

The *Echo* focuses on the Italian and Italian-American audience. The editor describes the editorial content as "Quality news features and arts reviews which focus on Italian or Italian-American subjects. Special regular features include (original) fashion photo essays, food column, humor and Op/Ed pieces. Once monthly, we research and present a look at one of the many Rhode Island ethnic neighborhoods."

The content of *Echo* attracts readers from other community groups, upscale professionals and fashion lovers.

With respect to flat fee payment for freelance articles, the editor indicates that extensive stories gain a higher fee. Photo payment is based on per assignment and per photo published. Contributors should check with editor if additional information is needed.

The editor also writes, "We stress the Italian-American focus of the newspaper, and give those stories first priority. Writers should remember that we appeal to a 35-45 year-old readership."

Italian-American	SASE: Required
AMERICAN CITIZEN ITALIAN PRESS, THE	English, ms.preference
Editor: Diana C. Failla	Query: Not necessary
13681 "V" Street	Ms.lgth.: 800-1200 wds.
Omaha	Pay: Negotiated/feature
Nebraska 68137	Photos/pay/credits
(402) 896-0403	Newspaper/Tabloid
Publisher: Diana C. Failla	Size: 11" x 17"
Established 1923	Black/white/color
Subscription: U.S.:$8; Intl.:$10	Newsprint paper
Distr.: Quarterly (See description)	Buff color paper
Cir.: U.S.(Iowa/Neb.): 49,000	Display
Italian, English text	Deadline: No response
10% non-English	Jewish-oriented readers
Freelance articles accepted	No "kill" fee

The American Citizen Italian Press, as described by the editor/publisher, contains news of political and international issues from abroad, local stories which are feature-oriented; e.g. business people in the community, and stories about the progress of Italian-Americans across the nation. There are also sections on sports, fashion, health, money matters, literature, restaurants and so forth.

Writer's Guidelines are available for contributors. These guidelines are thorough and indicate the periodical intends to be published bimonthly as of January 1989. These guidelines are a useful tool for those who wish to contribute to this publication. (Author's note: The guidelines are well-worth an SASE.)

Italian-American
L'AGENDA-The Italian-American News
Editor: Joseph Preite
26 Court Street
Brooklyn
New York 11242
(718) 875-0580
Publisher: Joseph Preite
Established 1969
Subscription: U.S.:$12
Distribution: Bimonthly
Circulation: U.S.:17,500
English text
2% non-English text
Freelance articles accepted

SASE: Not indicated
English ms.prefer
Query: Not indicated
No ms.length indicated
No payment
Photos/credits/no pay
Tabloid
Size: Not listed
Black/white/color
Newsprint paper
White color paper
Display ads
Deadline: Not listed
No outside group readers
No "kill" fee

L'Agenda, The Italian American News is a publication aimed at the Italian-American community.

The editor/publisher had no suggestions for contributors.

Italophiles
ATTENZIONE
Editor: Denise Gorga
152 Madison Ave; l5th Floor
New York
New York 10016
(212) 683-9000
Publisher: Adam Publications
Established 1979
Subscription: U.S.: $14.95
Distribution: Bimonthly
Cir.: U.S./Intl.:93,000 total
English, Italian text
0% to 1% non-English
Freelance articles accepted

SASE: Required
No ms.lang.preference
Query: Letter
No ms.length indicated
Pay/flat fee
Photos/credits/pay
Magazine
Size: Not listed
Black/white/color
Glossy paper
White color paper
Display ads
Deadline: Not listed
Outside readers: Italophiles
No "kill" fee

Attenzione is described by the editor as having a general interest which focuses on travel, food, the arts and Italian lifestyle.

The payment for freelance photographs varies.

No tips for contributors were given.

J

Japanese
NEW YORK NICHIBEI
Old Address:
27 Park Place
New York, New York 10007

The questionnaire was unclaimed and no forwarding address was available.

Japanese, Asian-American
PACIFIC CITIZEN
Acting Editor: J.K. Yamamoto
941 East 3rd. St.; 200
Los Angeles
California 90013
(213) 626-6936
Pub.:Japanese American Citizens League
Established 1929
Subscription: U.S.:$20;Intl.:$32
Distribution: Weekly
Circulation: U.S.:23,800; Intl.:120
English text
0% non-English
Freelance articles accepted

SASE: Required
English ms.preference
Query, letter
No ms.length indicated
Payment, flat fee
Photo/credits/flat fee
Tabloid
Size: Not listed
Black/white
Newsprint paper
White color paper
Display, classified
Deadline: Mon.bef.pub.
Libs., Congress
No "kill" fee

Pacific Citizen contains Asian-American community news with an emphasis on the Japanese American community. In addition to the ethnic group readers, there are libraries and politicians, including members of Congress, who receive the periodical.

According to the editor, *Pacific Citizen* publishes news articles on civil rights issues such as redress for Japanese-Americans interned during World War II, violence against Asian-Americans, job discrimination, university admissions of Asian-Americans and other subjects of related interest.

Feature sections focus on trends in Japanese American communities, interesting personalities, such as politicians, artists, and others, activities of Japanese American Citizens League, calendar items on upcoming community events, various columns and reviews.

For contributors, the editor writes, "Recommend looking over sample issues first to get an idea of content and format. Some familiarity with Japanese American or general Asian American community, history and current issues (is) needed."

(Cross-referenced: Asian-American)

Japanese-American
JAPAN AND AMERICA
Editor: J.L. Garner
Old address:
Pleasant Grove, Utah 84062

The questionnaire was returned and no forwarding address was available.

Jewish
AGENDA
Editor: Annette G. Jaffe
64 Fulton St.; No.1100
New York
New York 10038
(212) 227-5885
Publisher: New Jewish Agenda
Established December 1980
Subscription: U.S.:$15
Distribution: Quarterly
Circulation: U.S.: 3,000
Hebrew, Yiddish, English text
0%-1% non-English
No freelance/staff assigned

SASE: Not applicable
English ms.preference
Query: No response
No ms.length indicated
No payment
Photos/credits/pay
Newsletter
Size: 8.5" x 11"
Black/white
Paper: Regular 60 lb.
White color paper
No advertising
Deadline: Not listed
Libraries
"Kill" fee: Unknown

Agenda publishes information about Jewish culture, progressive Jews, and draws on the Talmudic teaching of tikkun olam, the just reordering of society, according to the editor.

The publication is described by the editor as "working for peace and social justice by applying Jewish religious and secular history and values to local organizing on current domestic and international concerns."

Among the many issues that *Agenda* addresses are the priority issues of peace and justice in the Middle East and Central America, feminism, disarmament, economic and social justice, lesbian and gay rights, and opposition to racism, anti-Semitism and apartheid.

The organization, New Jewish Agenda, which publishes this periodical has chapters in more than 45 American cities and has 5,000 members. The members work to foster traditional progressive Jewish values and to promote Jewish participation in progressive coalitions.

The non-profit organization is financed through individual memberships, donations and foundation grants, and all contributions are tax deductible.

For contributors, the editors comment: "Write well and type copy."

Jewish
AMERICAN JEWISH ARCHIVES
Editor: Abraham J. Peck
3101 Clifton Avenue
Cincinnati
Ohio 45215
(513) 221-1875
Publisher: American Jewish Archives
Established 1947
Sub.: U.S.:Controlled (complimentary)
Distribution: Semi-annual
Circulation: U.S.:4,500; International:500
English text
0% non-English
Freelance articles accepted

SASE: Required
English ms.preferred
Query, letter
No ms.length indicated
No pay
No photos/credits
Magazine
Size: 9" x 11"
Black/white
Newsprint paper
Buff color paper
No ads
Deadline: Unlisted
Universities
No "kill" fee

American Jewish Archives focuses on American Jewish studies. The articles are scholarly, and book reviews are included in the content of the publication.

The editor's tips for contributors: "Send for author's style sheet before writing article."

Jewish
AMERICAN JEWISH HISTORY
Eds: M.L. Raphael/N.M. Kaganiff
2 Thornton Road
Waltham
Massachusetts 02154
(617) 891-8110
Pub.: Amer.Jewish Historical Society
Established 1893
Sub.: U.S.:$50/yr.; Intl.:$50/yr.
Distribution: Not listed
Circulation: U.S.:3,375; Intl.:125
Yiddish, English text
2-3% non-English
Freelance articles accepted

SASE: Not required
No ms.lang.preferred
Query unnecessary
No ms.lgth.indicated
No payment
Photos/credits/no pay
Magazine
Size: Not listed
Black/white
Regular paper
Buff color paper
Display
Deadline: Unlisted
Outside group readers
No "kill" fee

American Jewish History publishes articles, book reviews and essays dealing with American Jewish history. In addition to Yiddish and English languages, the editor says German and Russian are used at "rare" times.

Jewish
AMERICAN JEWISH WORLD
Managing Editor: Stacey R. Bush
4509 Minnetonka Blvd.
Minneapolis
Minnesota 55416
(612) 920-7000
Publisher: Rabbi Marc N. Liebhaber
Established 1912
Subscription: U.S.:$16; Intl.:$21
Distribution: Weekly
Circulation: U.S.:7,000;Intl.:Minimal
Yiddish, Hebrew, English text
1% or less non-English
Freelance articles accepted

SASE: Required
Engl.ms.preference
Query, letter
No ms.length indicated
Pay/flat fee
Photos/credits
Newspaper
Size: 10" x 16"
Black/white/color
Newsprint paper
White color paper
Display, classified
Deadline:1 wk.bef. pub.
Christians, others
No "kill" fee listed

American Jewish World publishes information about international, national and local items of Jewish interest. The editor says, "That does not mean they (articles) all have to be "Jewish" per se, but should be of interest to our readers.

"We print a lot of material about Israel, obviously. We feel readers get, from one source, material they could only get if they also subscribed to several publications. Because we are not a daily, we tend to see news articles as offering insight or background to material that may have been in the daily paper earlier in the week.

"We make a strenuous effort not to favor any specific religious movement (Reform, Conservative or Orthodox), and feel we are good at printing all sides of any controversy."

The editor's tips for contributors:

"Articles should not appear elsewhere locally. They should be well-written, concise--shorter pieces are much more likely to be used. They must be on a topic we would be interested in; not general interest."

Jewish
AMERICAN ORT FEDERATION BULLETIN
Editor: Avi Feinglass
817 Broadway
New York
New York 10003
(212) 677-4400
Publisher: American ORT Federation
Established 1960
Subscription: Members only
Distribution: Quarterly
Circulation: Controlled
Hebrew, English text
.05% non-English
No freelance articles accepted

SASE: Not indicated
English ms.preference
Query: Not indicated
No ms.length indicated
No pay
No photos accepted
Tabloid
Size: 8.5" x 11"
Black/white/color
Glossy paper
White color paper
No advertising
Deadline: Not listed
No outside group readers
No "kill" fee listed

American ORT Federation Bulletin has Jewish interests, and publishes news of the organization.

The editor did not provide any tips for contributors.

Jewish
AMERICAN ORT FEDERATION YEARBOOK
Editor: Avi Feinglass
817 Broadway
New York
New York 10003
(212) 677-4400
Publisher: American ORT Federation
Established 1960
Subscription: Controlled
Distribution: Annual
Circulation numbers: Not listed
English text
0% non-English
No freelance articles accepted

SASE: No response
Ms.lang.: Unknown
Query: No response
No ms.lgth.indicated
Pay: No response
No photos/credits given
Magazine
Size: Not listed
Black/white/color
Glossy paper
White color paper
No advertising
Deadline: Not listed
No outside group rdrs.
No "kill" fee

American ORT Federation Yearbook is published annually for members of ORT and contains information about the organization.

No other information was provided.

Jewish
AMIT WOMAN
Editor: Micheline Ratzersdorfer
817 Broadway
New York
New York 10003
(212) 477-4720
Publisher: AMIT Woman
Established October 1932
Subscription: No response
Distribution: Five times/year
Circulation: U.S.:30,000
English text
0% non-English
Freelance articles accepted

SASE: Required
English ms.preference
Query unnecessary
No ms.lgth.indicated
Payment, flat fee
Photos/credits/no pay
Magazine
Size: 8.5" x 11"
Black/white, 1 color
Newsprint paper
White color paper
Display
Deadline: Not listed
No outside gp.readers
No "kill" fee

Amit Woman is written with a Jewish, Zionist and Traditional focus.

The editors prefer material clearly and intelligently written which conforms to Jewish religious law.

Jewish
ATLANTA JEWISH TIMES
Editor: Vida Goldgar
1575 Northside Dr.; P.O.Box 250287
Atlanta
Georgia 20325
(404) 355-6139
Publishers: Steve and Stan Rose
Established 1925
Sub.: U.S.:$28-33; Intl.:$65
Distribution: Weekly
Cir.: Total U.S./Intl.:7,300
English text
0% non-English
Freelance articles accepted

SASE: Not required
English ms.preference
Query, letter
No ms.length indicated
Payment/flat fee
Photos/credits
Tabloid
Size: 5 column width
Black/white/color
Newsprint paper
White color paper
Display, classified
Deadline: Tues.,5 p.m.
No outside group rdrs.
"Kill" fee paid

Atlanta Jewish News is an English language/Jewish interest newspaper which publishes news of local, national and international Jewish importance, opinion and commentaries.

The editor had no suggestions for contributors.

Jewish
B'NAI B'RITH STAR
Editor: Steve Schwartz
823 United Nations Plaza
New York
New York 10017
(212) 983-5800
Pub.:B'nai B'rith District One
Established 1950
Subscription: U.S.:Three/year
Distribution: Monthly
Circulation: U.S.:50,000 total
English text
0% non-English
Freelance articles accepted
SASE: Required
English ms.preference
Query, letter
No ms.length indicated
Payment: No response
Photos/credits
Newspaper
Size: 40 pages length
Black/white
Newsprint paper
White color paper
Display, classified
Deadline:10th & 15th of mo.
Outside readers: Unknown
"Kill" fee: No response

B'nai B'rith Star publishes news on B'nai B'rith District One which covers New York State and most of New England, with national news and some world events.

The editor says the publication has not been involved in much work with freelancers, but is very open to expansion.

Jewish
BOSTON JEWISH TIMES
Editor: J. Berkofsky
Old address:
Box 18427
Brooklyn, New York 11219

The questionnaire was unclaimed and no forwarding address was available.

Jewish
BUFFALO JEWISH REVIEW
Editor: A. Weiss
Old address
504 Frankhauser Road
Williamsville, New York 14221

The questionnaire was unclaimed and no forwarding address was available.

Jewish
CLEVELAND JEWISH NEWS
Editor: Cynthia Dettelbach
13910 Cedar Road
Cleveland
Ohio 44118
(216) 371-0800
Publisher: Cleveland Jewish Pub.Co.
Established May 29, 1964
Subscription: U.S.:$18; Intl.:$25
Distribution: Weekly
Circulation: U.S.:16,000; Intl.:53
English text
0% non-English
Freelance articles accepted

SASE: No response
English ms.preference
Query, letter
No ms.length indic.
Payment, flat fee
Photos/credits/pay
Tabloid
Size: Not listed
Black/white/color
Newsprint paper
Paper color: Unlisted
Display, classified
Deadline: Tues.,5 p.m.
No outside gp.readers
No "kill" fee

Cleveland Jewish News is an independent special interest paper that serves the Jewish Community of Cleveland. The editor had no tips for contributors.

Jewish
CONGRESS MONTHLY
Editor: Maier Deshell
15 E. 84th Street
New York
New York 10028
(212) 879-4500
Pub.: American Jewish Congress
Established 1933
Subscription: U.S.:$7.50; Intl.:$9
Distribution: Bimonthly
Circulation: U.S.:30,000
English text
0% non-English
Freelance articles accepted

SASE: Required
English ms.preference
Query, letter
No manuscript length indicated
Payment, by feature
Photos/credits/pay
Magazine
Size: 7" x 9.25"
Black/white/color
Newsprint paper
White color paper
Display
Deadline: 4 weeks before closing
Libs., schools, others
No "kill" fee

Congress Monthly publishes topics of concern to the Jewish community on a wide range of intellectual, involved Jewish views. The editor suggests that contributors write with authority and wit. According to the information sheets about this periodical, Congress Monthly is considered to be a magazine of opinion and Jewish Affairs.

In addition to answering the questionnaire developed for this study, the editor of *Congress Monthly* sent a concise and comprehensive packet of information about the publication.

Jewish
DAYTON JEWISH CHRONICLE
Editors: Anne Hammerman, Sam Rubin
118 Salem Ave.
Dayton
Ohio 45406
(513) 222-0783
Pub.: Dayton Jewish Chronicle/I.Seiden
Established 1962
Sub.: U.S.:$13(Dayton);Intl.:$15
Distribution: Weekly
Circulation: U.S.:1,300
English, occasional Yiddish text
0%-.5% non-English
Freelance articles accepted

SASE: Required
Eng. ms.preference
Query: No response
No ms.lgth.indicated
No pay; each reviewed
Photos/credits given
Tabloid
Size: Not listed
Black/white, some color
Newsprint paper
Paper color: Unlisted
Display, classified
Deadline: Mon.same week
Univ,libs,advertisers
No "kill" fee

According to the editor, the *Dayton Jewish Chronicle* deals with issues of interest to the Jewish community--both religious and secular.

The editor writes, "Our purpose is to inform the community of issues and events which have any bearing on its members, whether local, national or international.

"We have non-Jewish subscribers, and our publication goes to universities, libraries, other newspapers, as well as a variety of institutions and advertisers.

"We try not to repeat what the local dailies run and give more in-depth coverage to events that affect our ethnic community directly or indirectly."

Materials sent in by contributors is evaluated, and according to the editors, some of those items may be published if thought to be of interest to the readership. Every submitted item is judged on its own merit and not in comparison with other items. Newsworthiness, cost-effectiveness and available space are considered when evaluating submitted material, especially if the article has a time value.

Jewish
DETROIT JEWISH NEWS
News editor: Alan Hitsky
20300 Civic Center
Southfield
Michigan 48076
(313) 354-6060
Publisher: Charles Buerger
Established 1942
Sub.: U.S.:$24-26;Intl.:$38
Distribution: Weekly
Circulation: U.S.:18,000
English text
% non-English: No response
Freelance articles accepted

SASE: Required
English ms.preference
Query: Letter O.K.
No ms.length indicated
Payment/flat fee
Photos/credits/pay asgn.
Newspaper/tabloid
Size: Not listed
Black/white/color
Newsprint
White color paper
Display, classified
Deadline: Not listed
Outside group readers
"Kill" fee: No response

The *Detroit Jewish News* is Jewish-oriented. Articles of interest to the Detroit Jewish community are the focus of the editorial content.

The editor had no suggestions for contributors.

Jewish
HA'AM JEWISH NEWSMAGAZINE
Editor: Joel Mandel
112 Kerckhoff Hall;308 Westwood Pl.; UCLA
Los Angeles
California 90024
(213) 825-6280
Pub.: ASUCLA Communications Board
Established 1972
Subscription: No cost indicated
Distribution: Bimonthly
Circulation: U.S.:8,000
English text
0% non-English
Freelance articles accepted

SASE: Not indicated
Hebrew ms.preference
Query: No preference
No ms.length indicated
Pay: Column inches
Photos/credits/pay
Tabloid
Size: Not listed
Black/white/color
Newsprint paper
White color paper
Display
Deadline: Not listed
No outside group readers
"Kill" fee:Not listed

The ethnic interests of *Ha'am Jewish Newsmagazine* vary in cultural, religious and political Jewish topics. Additionally, information about student activities on the University of California-Los Angeles campus is published.

The editor had no tips for contributors.

Jewish
HERITAGE-S.W. JEWISH PRESS
Editor: Dan Brin
2130 S. Vermont Ave.
Los Angeles
California 90007
(213) 737-2122
Publisher: Herb Brin
Established 1914
Sub.: U.S.:$20-$25 (depends on edition)
Distribution: Weekly
Cir.: U.S.:39,000; Intl.:1,000
English text
0% non-English
Freelance articles accepted

SASE: Required
English ms.prefer
Query: No prefer
No ms.length indicated
Payment negotiated
Photos/credits/pay
Tabloid
Size: 14" length
B/W; color possible
Newsprint paper
Paper color: Unknown
Display, classified
Deadline: Friday
Pol., Christians
"Kill" fee: Not applicable

Heritage-Southwest Jewish Press editor says, "We're interested in Jewish news, (with) local and international news of interest to the broad Jewish community, (as well as) features and commentary."

For contributors, the editor says, "We need good material.

Jewish
INDIANA JEWISH HISTORY
Editor: Joseph Levine
203 West Wayne Street
Fort Wayne
Indiana 46802
(219) 422-3862
Pub.: Indiana Jewish History Society
Established 1973
Subscription: Not listed
Distribution: 1-2 issues/year
Circulation: U.S.:850 (Controlled)
English text
0% non-English
Freelance articles accepted

SASE: No response
English ms.preference
Query: No response
No ms.length indicated
No payment
Photos/credits
Magazine
Size: Not listed
Print color: Unknown
Newsprint paper
White color paper
Ads.: None
Deadline: Not listed
Libs.,history societies
No "kill" fee

The editor of *Indiana Jewish History* writes, "Our Society collects, preserves and publishes material dealing with the 200 years of Jewish life in Indiana. Our publication contains articles about individuals and organizations in Indiana."

The Society sends copies of its publication to libraries and other historical societies.

The editor's tips to contributors: "We ask our contributors to submit articles about Jews and/or Jewish life in Indiana."

Jewish
INSIDE MAGAZINE
Editor: Jane Biberman
226 So. 16th St.
Philadelphia
Pennsylvania 19102
(215) 893-5700
Publisher: Jewish Exponent Newspaper
Established 1980
Subscription: U.S.:$22
Distribution: Quarterly
Cir.: U.S.:80,000; Newsstand:10,000
English text
0% non-English
Freelance articles accepted

SASE: Required
English ms.preference
Query, letter
No ms.length indicated
Payment based on experience
Photos staff assigned
Magazine
Size: Not listed
Black/white/color
Glossy
Paper color: Not given
Display
Deadline: 1 mo.before pub.
City audience
"Kill" fee paid

Readers of *Inside Magazine* are described by the editor as "sophisticated, and the publication is a broad, general interest magazine for educated, upper-class readership interested in Jewish and general affairs." The editorial content, that is, the mixture of articles is described as "varied".

The editor listed no tips for contributors, but indicated that payment for photographs is calculated by the page size and credits are given.

Jewish
INTERMOUNTAIN JEWISH NEWS
Eds.: Miriam H.or Hillel Goldberg
1275 Sherman Street
Denver
Colorado 80203
(303) 861-2234
Publisher: Miriam H.Goldberg
Established 1913
Sub.: U.S.:$32; Intl.:$32
Distribution: Weekly
Cir.: U.S.:12,000; Intl.:Few
English text
% non-English: Minimal
Freelance accepted occasionally

SASE: No response
English ms.preference
Query, phone or letter
No ms.length indicated
Payment individually set
Photo/credits/pay negotiated
Tabloid
Size: 11"x 17"; and 10" x 16"
Black/white/color
Newsprint
White color paper
Display, classified
Deadline: Week before pub.
Libs.,ednl.inst.,others
"Kill" fee: Depends;ask editor

Intermountain Jewish News publishes local, national and international news along with analytical articles, human interest, special events and holiday stories in keeping with the interests of the readers. This means hard news, business and real estate and commercial news, entertainment, including interviews with visiting and community interest personalities. *Intermountain Jewish News* is described as having a solid editorial policy, letters to the editor, lively open forum, community and organization coverage along with a page of "light, airy news...small talk."

Payment for articles is negotiated, and payment of a "kill fee" for use of an idea depends upon the request. The editor mentioned that space is at a premium, so freelance articles are not used too often.

Freelance photographs may be used if they go with the article, and payment for photographs is individually negotiated.

Advertisement deadlines for camera ready materials is on Tuesdays.

With respect to tips for contributors, the editor says, "Strive for the highest standards in journalism, certainly to include the basics of proper spelling, pertinent subject or subject matter in a creative style. A thorough knowledge of material (is necessary), and don't become easily discouraged."

The editor provided a comprehensive information packet about the newspaper which permitted an in-depth review of the periodical and its offerings to the readership and contributors.

JEWISH CHICAGO
Old Address:
Jewish Chicago, Inc.
1800 W. Bernice
Chicago, Illinois 60613-2720.

The questionnaire was unclaimed and no forwarding address was available.

Jewish
JEWISH CIVIC PRESS
Editor: Abner L. Tritt
P.O. Box 15500
New Orleans
Louisiana 70175
(504) 895-8784, ext.5
Publisher: Abner L. Tritt
Established 1965
Sub.: U.S.:$5; Intl.:No information
Distribution: Monthly
Circulation: U.S.:8,000
English text
0% non-English
Freelance articles accepted

SASE: Required
English ms.preference
Query, letter
No ms.length indicated
No payment
Photos/credits
Tabloid
Size: Not listed
Black/white/color
Paper type: Unknown
Paper color: Unknown
Display, classified
Deadline: 3rd Friday of mo.
Businesses, religious orgs.
No "kill" fee

Jewish Civic Press, contains both Jewish and general news, but the editor says the content is mostly Jewish news.

As a writer's tip, the editor of suggests contributors prepare human interest copy with photos.

Jewish
JEWISH FRONTIER
Mg.Editor: Nahum Guttman
275 Seventh Avenue
New York
New York 10001
(212) 645-8121
Pub.: Labor Zionist Letters, Inc.
Established 1934
Sub.: U.S.:$15; CAN:$17.50; Others:$20
Distribution: Bi-monthly
Circulation: U.S.:4,500; Intl.:500
English text
0% non-English
Freelance articles accepted

SASE: No response
English ms.preference
Query: Letter O.K.
No ms.length indicated
Payment, by word
No photos (rarely used)
Magazine
Size: 8.5" x 11"
Black/white; Color cover
Paper type: No response
White color paper
Display;opt.classified
Deadline: 3 wks.bef.closing
Univ. & public libraries
No "kill" fee

Jewish Frontier describes its readership as people with a broad interest in state of Israel and Jewish affairs in U.S. and worldwide. The periodical treats American and worldwide political, socioeconomic, historical and cultural topics.

The editorial content focuses on current affairs, essays, poetry, memoirs, book reviews, Jewish history and political analysis.

Although the editors indicate a preference for English manuscripts, they will consider Yiddish or Hebrew manuscripts for translation.

Photos are rarely used.

The editors listed no suggestions or tips for contributors.

Jewish
JEWISH MONTHLY, THE
Editor: Marc Silver
1640 Rhode Island Ave.,N.W.
Washington
D.C. 20036
(202) 857-6645
Pub.: B'nai B'rith International
Established 1886
Subscription: U.S.:$8; Intl.:$23
Distribution: Monthly
Cir.: U.S.:160,000; Intl.:10,000
English text
0% non-English
Freelance articles accepted

SASE: Required
English ms.preference
Query, letter
No ms.length indicated
Payment, by word
Photos/credits
Magazine
Size: 8" x 10"
Black/white/color
Glossy paper
White color paper
Display, classified
Deadline: Not listed
Outside group readers
"Kill" fee: Not applicable

The ethnic interests of *The Jewish Monthly* are described by the editor as, "We look at the world from a Jewish perspective; (we) cover personalities, religion, culture, politics, lifestyles, trends and history of interest to a Jewish family audience." This description also outlines the editorial content of the publication.

The editor's tips to contributors: "Don't propose ideas without reading a copy of the magazine. We want stories that are lively and fresh, with a natural Jewish component. We are frequently sent immigrant reminiscences--while we try to cover our ethnic past, we prefer to concentrate on the present with an eye to the future. We value good, concise writing and would not consider a story that does not meet our editorial standards no matter how interesting the premise."

Jewish
JEWISH OBSERVER
Editor: Judith A. Rubenstein
P.O.Box 510
De Witt
New York 13214-0510
(315) 422-4104
Publisher: Syracuse Jewish Fed.,Inc.
Established 1978
Subscription: U.S.:$7; Intl:$25
Distribution: Bimonthly
Circulation: U.S.:5,800; Intl.:10
English text
0% non-English
Freelance articles accepted

SASE: Required
English ms.preference
Query: Unnecessary
Ms.length: 1,000 words
Payment/flat fee
Photos/credits
Tabloid
Size: Not listed
Black/white/color
Newsprint paper
White color paper
Display, classified
Deadline: 11 days before pub.
No outside group readers
"Kill" fee: No response

Jewish Observer publishes articles which deal with issues and events, local, national and international that are of interest and/or concern to the Jewish community.

The editor's tips for contributors: "Present an unusual angle or a topic; write in clear newspaper style.

"Send a cover letter that briefly tells me about the story and captures my interest immediately!

"Take the time to review *AP Stylebook*.

"Try to limit submissions in length to l,000 words--this is a newspaper, not a magazine."

Jewish
JEWISH PRESS
Editor: Morris Maline
333 South 132nd Street
Omaha
Nebraska 68154
(402) 334-8200
Pub.: Jewish Federation of Omaha
Established 1920
Sub.: U.S.:$18/yr.; Intl.:$25/year
Distribution: Weekly
Cir.: U.S.:3,890;Intl.:10
English text
0% non-English
Freelance articles accepted

SASE: Not required
English ms.prefer
Query unnecessary
No ms.length indicated
Pay: Flat fee; by col.inch
Photos/credits/pay
Newspaper
Size: 10.31" x 16"
Black/white/color
Newsprint paper
Paper color: Unknown
Display, classified
Deadline: Friday before pub.
Opinion leaders receive
No "kill" fee

The *Jewish Press* is described as a Jewish interest newspaper which publishes hard news, features and editorials.

The editor's tips to contributors are concise: "Desperately need quality photos."

Jewish
JEWISH PRESS, THE
Editor: Sholom Klass
338 Third Ave.
Brooklyn
New York 11215
(718) 330-1100
Pub.: Sholom Klass
Established March 1960
Subscription: U.S.:$30; Intl.:$45
Distribution: Weekly
Cir.: U.S.:165,000; Intl.:5,000
English text
0% non-English
Freelance articles accepted

SASE: Required
English ms.preference
Query with letter
No ms.length indicated
Payment; flat fee
Photos/pay/credits
Tabloid/newspaper
Size: Not listed
Black/white/color
Newsprint paper
White color paper
Display, classified
Deadline: Monday each week
Outside group readers
Pays "kill" fee

The Jewish Press publishes a variety of information such as Bible stories, also in cartoon form, news that pertains to Jewry, Israel, health, finance, and so forth.

The editorial content is described by the editor as "a storehouse of knowledge, news and entertainment."

"We usually publish 104 to 120 pages every week."

With respect to freelance articles received by this publication, the editor says, "Each article will be evaluated. It must have a Jewish or religious content."

Jewish
JEWISH STAR
Editor: Nevon Stuckey
109 Minna Street; Suite 323
San Francisco
California 94105-3701
(415) 421-4877
Publisher: Jewish Star
Established 1955
Subscription: U.S.:$12
Distribution: Bimonthly
Cir.: U.S.:1,750 (Controlled)
English text
0% non-English
No freelance articles accepted

SASE: Not applicable
Ms.lang.: Not applicable
Query : Not applicable
Ms.lgth.: Not applicable
Payment: Not applicable
Photos: Not applicable
Tabloid
Size: Not listed
Black/white
Newsprint paper
White color paper
Display, classified
Deadline: Not listed
No outside group readers
"Kill fee": Not applicable

Jewish Star publishes information about Jewish news in Israel and the United States, and the editor describes the editorial content as "independent."

No tips for contributors were given as this publication does not accept any freelance articles.

Jewish
JEWISH TRANSCRIPT, THE
Editor: Craig Degginger
1904 3rd Ave; 510 Securities Bldg.
Seattle
Washington 98101
(206) 624-0136
Publisher: Consolidated Press
Established March 6, 1924
Subscription: U.S.:$12
Distribution: Twice monthly
Circulation: U.S.:4,000; Intl.:12
English text
0% non-English
Freelance articles accepted

SASE: Required
English ms.preference
Query: No preference
No ms.lgth.indicated
Payment/flat fee
Photos/credits/no pay
Tabloid
Size: Not listed
Black/white/color
Newsprint paper
White color paper
Display, classified
Deadline: 10 days before pub.
No outside group readers
"Kill" fee: No response

The Jewish Transcript describes the interests of its readers as people interested in news about the Jewish community. This includes local, national and international news.

Jewish
JWVA BULLETIN
Editor: I. Halperin
Old address:
1712 New Hampshire Ave.N.W.
Washington, D.C. 20009

The questionnaire was unclaimed and no forwarding address was available.

Jewish
LIFELINES (NEW YORK)
Editors: N.Laufer/N.Thorn
Old address:
8 W. 40th Street
New York, New York 10018

The questionnaire was unclaimed and no forwarding address was available.

Jewish
M'GODOLIM: A JEWISH MAGAZINE
Editor: S.Ben-Israel
Old address:
2921 E. Madison St.; Ste.7 BSD
Seattle, Washington 98112

The questionnaire was returned and no forwarding address was available.

Jewish
MACHLOKET (Originally: Shining Star)
Editor: Richard Newman
Interfaith Center/SUNY
Stony Brook
New York 11794-5335
(516) 632-6565
Pub.: B'nai B'rith Hillel Foundation
Established 1981
Subscription: U.S.:$0; Intl.:$0
Distribution: Quarterly
Circulation: U.S.:4,995; Intl.:5
English, occ. Hebrew text
% non-English: No response
Freelance articles accepted

SASE: Not required
English ms.prefer
Query: No preference
No ms.lgth.indicated
No payment
Photos/credits/no pay
Tabloid
Size: 11" x 22"
Black/white
Newsprint paper
White color paper
Display ads
Deadline: Not listed
Libraries, univ.,administrators
No "kill" fee

Originally named *Shining Star*, this periodical is now titled, *Machloket*, and its readership is described as being interested in Jewish cultural, social, political and religious issues and events which concern the Jewish community on the campus at State University of New York (SUNY)-Stony Brook.

Although the *Machloket* publishes in English, occasional Hebrew is used for poetry, etc., but a translation is always provided.

Editorial content addresses important issues that face the Jewish community, but with diverse views represented.

The editor writes, "Contributors should submit articles which are of relevant interest to Jewish readers, be lucid and articulate."

Jewish
MOMENT MAGAZINE
Assistant Ed.: K. Persellin
678 Massachusetts Ave.; Ste.903
Cambridge
Massachusetts 02139
(617) 354-2121
Publisher: Leonard Fein
Established June 1975
Subscription: U.S.: $27
Distribution: Monthly
Cir.: U.S.:23,799; Intl.:0
English, Hebrew, Yiddish text
1% non-English
Freelance articles accepted

SASE: Required
English ms.preference
Query, no prefer.,letter O.K.
Ms.length: 3,000 words optimum
Pay: Story and/or length
Photos/credits/payment
Magazine
Size: Not listed
Black/white/color
Newsprint paper
White color paper
Display, classified
Deadline: Not listed
Interested in Jewish issues
Kill"fee: No response

Moment is a Jewish cultural magazine that focuses on domestic policy, Israel, religious issues, recent fiction and Soviet Jewry. Readers from outside the group include anyone interested in current issues and events in the Jewish community.

In addition to the subjects listed above, *Moment* publishes cultural, historical, political, life-style oriented articles, "think pieces," occasional poetry and short stories.

Different article lengths are appropriate for different articles, therefore, editors prefer to have manuscript length at an optimal 3,000 words.

Jewish
NA'AMAT WOMAN
Editor: Judith A. Sokoloff
200 Madison Ave.; Suite 1808
New York
New York 10016
(212) 725-8010
Publisher: NA'AMAT USA
Established 1925
Subscription: U.S.:$5; Intl.:$15
Distribution: Five/year (begin Jan.)
Circulation: U.S.:28,300; Intl.:700
English, Hebrew, Yiddish text
6% non-English
Freelance articles accepted

SASE: Required
English ms.preferred
Query: No preference
No ms.length indicated
Payment/by word
Photos/credits/pay
Magazine
Size: Not listed
Black/white
Newsprint paper
White color paper
Display
Deadline: Varied
Inter-faith organizations
"Kill" fee: No response

Na'Amat Woman is, according to the editor, "geared to the Jewish community."

Articles cover a wide variety of subjects, including political, social and women's issues, arts, literature, Israel, activities of Na'Amat (Movement of Working Women and Volunteers) in Israel. Fiction and book reviews are a part of this publication.

The editor advises contributors that "No poetry is accepted." (Emphasis by editor of *Na'Amat Woman*.)

Jewish
NCJW JOURNAL
Editor: Michele Spirn
15 East 26th Street
New York
New York 10010
(212) 532-1740
Pub.: National Council Jewish Women
Established 1950s
Subscription: U.S.:$2
Distribution: Quarterly
Circulation: U.S.:100,000
English text
0% non-English
No freelance articles accepted

SASE: Not applicable
English ms.preferred
Query: Not applicable
No ms.length indicated
No pay: Staff assigned
No freelance photos
Magazine
Size: 8.5" x 11"
Black/white/color
Glossy paper
White color paper
Display
Deadline: Not listed
Outside group readers
"Kill" fee: Unknown

NCJW Journal, published by the National Council of Jewish Women, contains articles which describe the projects and programs of the NCJW. The editor says people interested in child care, women's issues, constitutional rights, and aging also read the journal. Additionally, articles of interest to NCJW members about specific projects and programs of the organization are included in the journal.

The editor had no specific tips for contributors.

Jewish
RESPONSE
Eds.: L.Triantopoulos, Rabbi Cooper
9760 W. Pico Blvd.
Los Angeles
California 90035
(213) 553-9036
Publisher: Simon Wiesenthal Center
Established: No date given
Subscription: Not applicable
Distribution: Quarterly
Circulation: U.S.:350,000
English text
0% non-English
No freelance: Staff assigned

SASE: Not applicable
English ms.prefer
Query: Not applicable
No ms.length indicated
Pay: Not applicable
Photos: Staff assigned
Magazine
Size: Not listed
Black/white/color
Paper type: Not listed
White color paper
No advertising
Deadline: Not applicable
Outside group readers
"Kill" fee: Not applicable

Response magazine is geared to a Jewish readership. Areas of concern include the upsurge of neo-Nazism, prosecution of Nazi war criminals, and education on the Holocaust.

This periodical focuses on the Simon Wiesenthal Center's social action in the areas of anti-Semitism, Soviet Jewry, neo-Nazis and Nazi war criminals. Scholarly publications of the Center's Holocaust-related topics and reports come from department heads and the Center's branches are featured.

As the contents of this publication are assigned to staff members, no freelance manuscripts or photographs are accepted.

Jewish	SASE: No information
ROCKY MOUNTAIN JEWISH HISTORICAL NOTES	English ms.preferred
Editor: John Livingston	Query: No preference
Center for Judaic Studies	No ms.length indic.
University of Denver	No pay
Denver, Colorado 80208	Photos/credits
(303) 871-3022	Magazine
Pub.: Rocky Mtn.Jewish Historical Soc.	Size: Not listed
Established 1977	Black/white
Subscription: Rate not listed	Paper type: Unknown
Distribution: Quarterly	Buff color paper
Circulation: U.S.: 600	Ads: Unknown
English text	Deadline: Unknown
0% non-English	No outside gp.rdrs.
Freelance articles accepted	"Kill" fee: Unknown

Rocky Mountain Jewish Historical Notes publishes information about all aspects of Jewish history in the Rocky Mountain region, and the editorial content is listed as scholarly.

The editor did not give any tips for contributors, but contributors would probably benefit by reviewing a copy of the publication prior to sending articles for consideration by the editor.

Jewish
RUTGERS JEWISH PERSPECTIVES
Editorial Board
126 College Ave; Box 43
New Brunswick
New Jersey 08901
No telephone listed
Pub.:Rutgers Jewish Per.Studies Gp.
Established: No date given
Subscription: U.S.:$5; Intl.:$5
Distribution: Quarterly
Circulation: U.S.:3,000; Intl.:0
English, some Hebrew text
1-2% non-English
Freelance articles accepted

SASE: Not required
English ms.preferred
Query: No preference
No ms.length indicated
No payment
Photos/credits/no pay
Tabloid
Size: Not listed
Black/white/color
Paper: Not specified
White color paper
Display
Deadline: 1 month before pub.
Outside group readers
"Kill" fee: No response

Rutgers Jewish Perspectives publishes news with a definite Jewish interest from the national or the local scene.

The editor's tips to contributors: "We accept anything relating to Jewish Campus or national interests, as long as it's typed."

Jewish
SH'MA: A JOURNAL OF JEWISH RESPONSIBILITY
Editor: Eugene B. Borowitz
P.O.Box 567
Port Washington
New York 11050
(516) 944-9791
Publisher: SH'MA, Inc.
Established November 1970
Subscription: U.S.:$12; Intl.:$12
Dist.: Biweekly; except June, July, August
Circulation: Not given
English text
% non-English used: Not listed
Freelance articles accepted

SASE: Required
English ms.prefer
Query unnecessary
Ms.lgth.: Ask editor
Pay: 25 copies
No photos
Newsletter
Size: 8" x 10"
Black/white
Glossy paper
White color paper
No ads
Deadline: Unknown
Other religious gps.
No "kill" fee

SH'MA--A Journal of Jewish Responsibility is described by the editor as a forum for civilized debate on matters confronting the Jewish community. The editor also says opposing Jewish views are brought into direct, but civil confrontation, in this publication.

Outside group readers and subscribers include interested members of other religious groups.

SH'MA publishes information on issues that range from medical ethics and the nuclear arms race to Jewish traditions, modernity and humor. This publication is described as provocative, candid and lively.

Writers for the scholarly and the general audience would benefit from reviewing a copy of this publication prior to submitting manuscripts.

Jewish
SHABBOT SHALOM
Editor: Clifford Goldstein
6840 Eastern Ave. N.W.
Washington
D.C. 20012
(207) 722-6000
Pub.: No.Am.Div.Seventh Day Adventists
Established 1954
Sub.: U.S.:$4.95; Intl.:$6.95
Distribution: Quarterly
Circulation: U.S.:8,400; Intl.:100
English text
0% non-English
Freelance articles accepted

SASE: Not required
English ms.preferred
Query: Send to editor
No ms.lgth.indicated
Payment
Photos
Newsprint paper
Size: Not listed
Black/white/color
Newsprint paper
Color paper: Unknown
No ads
Deadline: Unknown
Christian readers
No "kill" fee

Shabbot Shalom editors describe their readers as mostly Jewish, but also list some Christians among subscribers.

The content of this periodical is classified as political, religious, social, medical and historical.

For contributors, the editor writes, "Send query to me."

Jewish
WESTERN STATES JEWISH HISTORY
Editor: Norton B. Stern
2429-23rd St.
Santa Monica
California 90405
(213) 450-2946
Pub.:Western States Jewish Hist.Assoc.
Established October 1968
Sub.: U.S.:$15; Intl.:$17
Distribution: Quarterly
Circulation: Not listed
English text
0% non-English
Freelance articles accepted

SASE: Required
English ms.preference
Query unnecessary
No ms.length listed
No payment
Photos/credits/no pay
Magazine
Size: 6" x 9"
Black/white
Paper type: No response
White color paper
No advertising
Deadline: Not listed
Univ.,foreign libs.,hist.,socio.
"Kill fee": No response

Western States Jewish History describes its readership as interested in anything with some connection to Jewish life and interests.

This periodical is sent to all major American university libraries, American historical societies, and foreign libraries including those in Israel.

A regular editor's page and "Periodical Reflections" section are included in the publication.

The editor suggests that contributors review a copy of the publication before submitting articles. All materials submitted must be fully and carefully documented.

Jewish	SASE: Required
WM.PETSCHEK NATL.JEWISH FAMILY CTR.NSLTR.	English ms.prefer
Editor: Lawrence Grossman	Query, letter
165 E. 50th St.	No ms.lgth.indic.
New York	No payment
New York 10022	Photo/pay/credits
(212) 751-4000	Tabloid
Publisher: American Jewish Committee	Size: Not listed
Established 1980	Black/white/color
Subscription: Controlled	Paper: Not listed
Distribution: Quarterly	White color paper
Circulation: U.S.:4,500; Intl.:500	Ads: Not listed
English text	Deadline: Unknown
0% non-English	Christian readers
Freelance articles accepted	"Kill" fee: No rep.

The *William Petschek National Jewish Family Center Newsletter* addresses Jewish family issues and is supportive of families with a broad definition of family forms, according to the editor.

The editor suggests that contributors look at previous issues of the *Newsletter* to see the kinds of issues the publication addresses.

Jewish
ZEIREI FORUM
Editor: Eliezer Gervirtz
84 Williams Street
New York
New York 10038
(212) 797-9000
Pub.: Zeirei Agudath Israel of America
Established 1971
Subscription: U.S.:$7; Intl.:$12
Distribution: Quarterly
Circulation: U.S.:4,000
English text
0% non-English
Freelance articles accepted

SASE: Required
English ms.prefer
Query:Unnecessary
No ms.lgth.indic.
No payment
Photos/credits only
Magazine
Size: Not listed
Black/white
Regular paper
White color paper
Display
Deadline: Unlisted
Libraries receive
No "kill" fee

Zeirei Forum is a publication that addresses Orthodox Jewish interests. The editor describes the content of the publication as "articles of popular and scholarly interest relative to Jews and Judaism."

The editor provided no tips to contributors.

Jewish (Holocaust)
DIMENSIONS:A JOUR.OF JEWISH HOLOCAUST STUD.
Editor: Dennis B. Klein
823 United Nations Plaza
New York
New York 10017
(212) 490-2525
Pub.: Anti-Defamation Leag.B'nai B'rith
Established 1985
Subscription: U.S.:$12;Intl.:$15
Distribution: Tri-annual
Circulation: U.S.:9,500; Int:500
English; some German, French text
1% non-English
Freelance articles accepted

SASE: Required
Eng.ms.prefer
Query, letter
No ms.lgth.indic.
Pay/flat fee
Photos/pay arr.
Magazine
Size: 8.5" x 11"
Black/white/color
Glossy paper
White color pap.
Display ads
Deadline:S.,D.,J.
Outside readers
"Kill"fee: Unk.

Dimensions: A Journal of Holocaust Studies is, according to the editor, aimed at all interests with special interest for Jewish readers.

The editor says of the publication: "Aimed at compelling new ways of thinking and teaching about the Holocaust. Special focus on the impact of the Holocaust on contemporary societies and cultures."

With respect to tips for contributors the editor says, "New ideas, clear writing, interpretive and analytical and general interest."

Jewish (Holocaust)
MARTYRDOM AND RESISTANCE
Editor: Harvey Rosenfeld
48 West 37th St.
New York
New York 10018
(212) 564-1865
Pub.: Martyrdom/Resistance Foundation
Established 1974
Subscription: Controlled
Distribution: Bimonthly
Cir.: U.S.:20,000; Intl.:1,000
English text
0% non-English
Freelance articles accepted

SASE: Unnecessary
English ms. prefer
Query unnecessary
No ms.length indicated
No payment
Photos/credits/no pay
Newspaper
Size: 11.5" x 15
Black/white
Newsprint paper
White color paper
No advertising
Deadline: Unlisted
Orgs., schools, ed.
No "kill" fee

Martyrdom and Resistance is written for all of those people interested in the Holocaust, and includes news and features related to the Holocaust and the remembrance of it.

Prospective writers are encouraged to look at the format and write to the editor.

Jewish, American
AMERICAN JEWISH ARCHIVES
Editor: Abraham J. Peck
3101 Clifton Avenue
Cincinnati
Ohio 45215
(513) 221-1875
Pub.: American Jewish Archives
Established 1947
Subscription: Controlled
Distribution: Semi-annual
Circulation: U.S.:4,500; Intl.:500
English text
0% non-English
Freelance articles accepted

SASE: Required
English ms.preference
Query necessary
No ms.length indicated
No payment
No photos/credits/no pay
Magazine
Size: 9" x 11"
Black/white
Newsprint paper
Buff color paper
Ads: No response
Deadline: No response
Universities
No "kill" fee

American Jewish Archives focuses on American Jewish studies with scholarly articles and book reviews.

The editor asks that contributors request a copy of *Author's Style Sheet* before writing or sending articles to be considered for publication. (Author's note: Remember: Enclose an SASE.)

Jewish, American
GREATER PHOENIX JEWISH NEWS
Mg.Editor: Levi Reiss
P.O. Box 26590
Phoenix
Arizona 85068
(602) 870-9470
Pub.: Phoenix Jewish News, Inc.
Established 1948
Subscription: U.S.:$22;Intl.:$50
Distribution: Weekly
Circulation: U.S.:5,994;Intl.:6
English text
0% non-English
Freelance articles accepted

SASE: Required
English ms.prefer
Query unnecessary
No ms.length indicated
Pay by column inch
Photos/credits/pay
Tabloid
Size: 11" x 14"
Black/white/color
Newsprint paper
Buff color paper
Display, classified
Deadline: Mon.,9 days bef.pub.
Libs.,govt.,local business
"Kill" fee: No response

Greater Phoenix Jewish News editor describes the periodical's audience as an "American Jewish readership, well-educated, well-read, interested in local, national and international Jewish concerns."

The contents include local features, news, social and cultural events, further described by the editor as "cradle to grave," with national, international analysis of issues and events of particular interest to and with an impact on Jews.

The editor suggests that contributors submit only high quality pieces that invite reader interest and involvement. The editor writes, "We are particularly anxious to consider articles that address the concerns of younger Jewish families, especially lifestyle pieces."

Jewish, American
LEADER'S DIGEST
Editor: No listing
165 E. 56th St.
New York
New York 10022
No telephone listing
Pub.: American Jewish Committee
Established: Date not given.
Cir.: Controlled/In-House pub.
Distribution: Five times/year
Circulation: U.S.:4,000
Language text: Unknown
% non-English: Unknown
No freelance accepted

SASE: Unknown
Ms.lang.prefer: Unknown
Query: Not applicable
Ms length: Unknown
Pay: Unknown
Photos: Unknown
Format: Unknown
Size: Unknown
Print Process: Unknown
Paper type: Unknown
Paper color: Unknown
Ad Type: Unknown
Deadline: Unknown
Outside readers: None
"Kill" fee: Unknown

Leader's Digest is an in-house membership publication and not available to the general audience.

Jewish, American
PRESENT TENSE
Editor: Murray Polner
165 East 56 Street
New York
New York 10022
(212) 751-4000
Pub.: American Jewish Committee
Established 1973
Sub.:U.S.:$18;Intl.: Request info.
Distribution: Bimonthly
Circulation: U.S.:45,000
English text
% non-English: No response
Freelance articles accepted

SASE: Required
English ms.preference
Query, letter
No ms.lgth.indicated
Pay: Negotiated
Photos/credits/pay
Magazine
Size: Not listed
Black/white/color
Glossy paper
White color paper
Display ads
Deadline: No response
Outside group readers
Kill" fee: Not applicable

The ethnic interests of *Present Tense* are described as American Jewish. The non-ethnic audience is said to have similar interests as the editor writes that the issues addressed are those which concern Americans.

The editor says the publication is independent and concerned with life throughout the world.

Aside from advising potential contributors to query first, the editor writes, "Read the magazine BEFORE querying!!" (The emphasis is by the editor of *Present Tense.*)

Jewish, Secular
JEWISH CURRENTS
Editor: Morris V. Schappes
22 E. 17th St.; Suite 601
New York
New York 10003
(212) 924-5740
Pub.: Assoc.Promote Jewish Secularism
Established 1946
Subscription: U.S.:$15; Intl.:$18
Distribution: Monthly
Circulation: U.S.:3,629; Intl.: None
English text
0% non-English
Freelance articles accepted

SASE: Required
English ms.prefer
Query unnecessary
No ms.length indicated
No payment
Photos, no credits/pay
Magazine
Size: 5.5" x 8.5"
Black/white
Paper: Regular, coated
White color paper
Display
Deadline: 8 weeks bef.pub.
Univ.and other libraries
No "kill" fee

Jewish Currents concentrates on secular, not religious, content with special interest in Yiddish history, culture and literature. It is described as politically progressive with interests in the Jewish social-ethical tradition. Special attention is given to Black-Jewish relations, the Holocaust and the Soviet-Jewish situation.

No suggestions given for contributors.

Jewish, Secular
WORKMEN'S CIRCLE CALL, THE
Editor: Walter L. Kirschenbaum
45 East 33rd Street
New York
New York 10002
(212) 889-6800
Publisher: The Workmen's Circle
Established 1936
Cir.: Controlled, membership
Distribution: Five times/year
Circulation: U.S.:50,000
English, occ. Yiddish text
.5% ('if that' writes the editor) non-English
No freelance articles accepted

SASE: Not applicable
English manuscript prefer
Query, letter
Ms.length: Not applicable
Pay: Not applicable
Photos/credits/pay
Tabloid
Size: Not listed
Black/white/color
Newsprint paper
White color paper
Display, classified
Deadline: 2 wks.bef.pub.
AFL-CIO, Civil Rts.leaders
"Kill" fee: Not applicable

The Workmen's Circle Call is a secular Jewish publication with anti-totalitarian, pro-labor, pro-Israel (without Zionist affiliations), stance.

The Jewish fraternal organization was formed by immigrants in 1900 and retained concern for Yiddish cultural heritage and social progressivism. The organization is considered non-partisan, but has strong ties of past existence with social-democratic affinities through the labor movement (AFL-CIO).

The publication reflects the general purpose of organization with articles offering a variety of dissent.

Jewish, Southern Jewry
SOUTHERN JEWISH WEEKLY
Editor: Isadore Moscovitz
P.O. Box 3297
Jacksonville
Florida 32206
(904) 634-1469
Pub.: Isadore Moscovitz
Established 1924
Subscription: U.S.:$10
Distribution: Weekly
Cir.: U.S.:980; Intl:10
English text
0% non-English
Freelance articles accepted

SASE: Required
English ms.preference
Query: No preference
No ms.length indicated
Pay for news, features
Photos/credits/pay
Tabloid
Size: Not listed
Black/white: 90%; Color: 10%
Newsprint
White color paper
Display, classified
Deadline: This wk.for next wk.
Bible students & churches
No "kill" fee

Southern Jewish Weekly contains news of interest to the Jewish readership, especially to Southern Jewry, according to the editor's description of the publication. The publication is also described as pro-Israel and dedicated to democracy.

The editor's tips to contributors: "Type neatly, accurately, double-space, keep articles brief and send SASE for return of articles or checks."

Jewish, Zionist
HADASSAH MAGAZINE
Exec.Editor: Alan M. Tigay
50 West 58th Street
New York
New York 10019
(212) 303-8014
Pub.: Hadassah; Women's Zion.Org.
Established 1914
Sub.: U.S.:$1.50/issue(Controlled)
Distribution: Ten issues/year
Cir.: U.S.:360,000; International:0
English text
0% non-English
Freelance articles accepted

SASE: Required
English ms.preference
Query, letter
No ms.length indicated
Pay/fl.fee;most articles asgn.
Photos/pay/credits
Magazine
Size: 8.5" x 11"
Black/white/color
Glossy paper
White color paper
Display, classified
Deadline:18th of sec.mo.bef.pub.
Libraries
No "kill" fee

Hadassah Magazine is published by Hadassah, a women's Zionist Jewish organization, therefore, the magazine's interests focus primarily on Jewish life in America and Israel.

The editor of *Hadassah Magazine* writes: "We have regular columns on political questions that affect Jews in America and Israel, Jewish parenting, travel and the arts. There is a regular column on the Hadassah-Hebrew University Hospital in Jerusalem and a book review section for fiction and non-fiction that deals with Jewish topics. We use two to three feature length articles per month and accept short fiction as well."

Payment for freelance articles and photographs is given, although freelance photographs are rarely accepted since most are assigned. Cover photographs (color transparency) payment is $175; Black and White inside: $50 and $30 for each additional photo in one article. Check with the editor regarding selection and payment rate policies on freelance photographs.

(Cross-referenced: Zionist.)

Jewish, Zionist
HERZL INSTITUTE BULLETIN
Editor
515 Park Avenue
New York
New York 10022
No phone listing
Publisher: Theodor Herzl Institute
Established: No date given.
Sub.: Member: Individual:$20; Couple:$35
Distribution: Biweekly
Circulation: No information
English text
%non-English: No response
Freelance articles not accepted

SASE: No information
Ms.lang.: No response
Query: See description
No ms.length indicated
Payment: Unknown
Photos used
Size: 7" x 10"
Bulletin
Black/white
Bond paper
White color paper
No ads
Deadline: Not listed
No outside group readers
"Kill fee": No response

The *Herzl Institute Bulletin* and *Seasonal Preview* booklet are published by The Theodor Herzl Institute. The Institute's purpose and policy, published in the *Seasonal Preview* booklet states:

> "The Theodor Herzl Institute, sponsored by the World Zionist Organization-American Section, is a center for adult Zionist education. Through a wide range of educational activities, the Institute fosters a greater understanding of contemporary Jewish problems here and abroad, examines the values and precepts of the Jewish Heritage, encourages the study of modern Israel, and engages in social research in areas of Jewish interest.
>
> "The spirit of free inquiry guides all Institute activities. It is bound by no commitment to any particular Zionist ideological orientation. The scope of its work encompasses the broad range of Jewish interests, with particular consideration given to the history and impact of Zionism--the national liberation movement of the Jewish people, which culminated in the creation of the State of Israel."

According to the response to the questionnaire, queries should pertain to membership information or program offerings only. Respondent requested that no other queries be sent.

(Cross-referenced: Zionist.)

Jews of Spanish or Afro-Asian Descent
AMERICAN SEPHARDI
Editor: M. Mitchell Serels
500 W. 185th St.
New York
New York 10033
(212) 960-5235
Publisher: Yeshiva University
Established 1969
Subscription: U.S.:$10; Intl.:$10
Distribution: Irregular
Circulation: U.S.:5,000; Intl.:2,500
English, Hebrew, French, Spanish text
% non-English varies
Freelance articles accepted

SASE: No response
No ms.lang.preferred
Query, letter
No ms.length indicated
No payment
Photos accepted
Magazine
Size: Not listed
Black/white
Paper type: Unknown
Buff color paper
Advertising: None
Deadline: Unlisted
Academic institutions
No "kill" fee

American Sephardi addresses an audience of Sephardic-Jewish people of Spanish or Afro-Asian descent.

The editor's tips for contributors: "Must be high quality academic articles and related photographs."

According to the editor, *American Sephardi* is published on an "irregular" basis.

Jicarilla Apache
JICARILLA CHIEFTAN
Editors: M.F. Polanco & V.L. Vigil
P.O. Box 507
Dulce
New Mexico 87528-0507
(505) 759-3242
Publisher: Jicarilla Apache Tribe
Established 1961
Sub.:U.S.in-co$12;out of county: $28;Intl.:$24
Distribution: Biweekly
Circulation: U.S.:1,100 total
English, some Jicarilla
.06% non-English
Freelance articles accepted

SASE: Not indicated
No ms.lang.preferred
Query, letter only
No ms.length indicated
No payment
Photos/credits
Tabloid
Size: 5 col.wide x 13"
Black/white/color
Regular paper
Paper color: Unknown
Display, classified
Deadline: Mon.after pub.
Univ.,coll.libs.,pol.
No "kill" fee

Jicarilla Chieftain contains information about Jicarilla Apaches, other news which would have an impact on the people and the region, and national news of Native Americans. The editors describe their publication as containing information that will inform, educate and enhance the life style of the readership.

For prospective contributors, the editors give the following information: "Timely information on Native American issues that will be of interest to our readers."

(Cross-referenced: Apache.)

K

Korean
KORAN CULTURE
Editor: Laurence J. Pett
5505 Wilshire Blvd.
Los Angeles
California 90036
(213) 936-7141
Pub.: Korean Cultural Service Consul.Gen.
Established 1980
Subscription: U.S.:$0 (free)
Distribution: Quarterly
Circulation: U.S.:13,000
English text
0% non-English
No freelance accepted

SASE: Required
English ms.preferred
Query, letter
No ms.length indicated
Pay if ms.accepted
Photos/credits
Magazine
Size: 8.5" x 10.5"
Black/white/color
Glossy paper
White color paper
No advertising
Deadline: Unlisted
Some outside readers
No "kill" fee

Korean Culture is available to anyone who is interested in Korean culture.

Articles about Korean art, history and culture are the focus of this magazine.

The editor's tips for contributors: "Read the magazine or inquire of editor for guidelines."

L

Latin
LATIN NEW YORK
Editor: I. Sanabria
Old address
316 Fifth Ave.; Ste. 301
New York, New York 10001

The questionnaire was unclaimed and no forwarding address was available.

Latin American, So.American, Cuban
LA TRIBUNA DE NORTH JERSEY
Editor: Humberto Perez
70 Kossuth Street
Newark
New Jersey 07101
(201) 589-3742
Publisher: Carlos Bidot
Established March 11, 1962
Subscription: U.S.:$25 (Controlled)
Distribution: Bimonthly
Circulation: U.S.:50,000 (total)
Spanish text
100% non-English
Freelance articles acc./Agent refer.

SASE: Required
Spanish ms.preference
Query, letter
No ms.length indicated
No payment
Photos/cr./no pay
Tabloid
Size: Not listed
B/W; Color special ed.
Paper type: Not listed
White color paper
Display, classified
Deadline: Not listed
Colleges, businesses
No "kill" fee

La Tribuna de North Jersey publishes information for the Cuban exile community, Latin Americans and South Americans in the United States. The primary focus of the editorial content is human rights against dictatorship and against Communism.

The editor provided no tips for contributors.

(Cross-referenced: Latin American, South American and Cuban.)

Latin-American, Spanish
HISPANIC JOURNAL
Editor: Joseph B. Spieker
456 Sutton Hall; Indiana U.of Pa.
Indiana
Pennsylvania 15705
(412) 357-2327
Pub.: Dept.Spanish/Class.Languages
Established Fall 1979
Sub.: U.S.&Intl.:$8 indiv./inst.$12
Distribution: Biannual
Cir.: U.S.:400; Intl.: 200
Spanish, English, Portuguese, Catalan
50% non-English
Freelance articles accepted

SASE: Not required
Spanish, English ms.prefer
Query: Not required
No ms.lgth.indicated
No payment
No photos/pay/credits
Magazine
Size: 8.75" x 5.75"
Black/white
Glossy paper
White color paper
No ads
Deadline: Not listed
Profs., univ.libraries
No "kill" fee

Hispanic Journal publishes, according to the editor, "articles examining primarily literary works of the Spanish and Latin American cultures which includes language,linguistics, history, art and culture of Hispano-America."

Although approximately half of the journal is published in Spanish, English is the other primary language. Some Portuguese and Catalan languages are used in the periodical. The editor says the length of the journal is from 150-200 pages.

The editor advises contributors to follow the *MLA Style Sheet* guidelines when submitting manuscripts for consideration.

(Cross-referenced: Spanish.)

Latino, Chicano
EL TECOLOTE NEWSPAPER
Editor: Carlos Alcala
P.O. Box 40037
San Francisco
California 94140
(415) 824-7878
Publisher: Accion Latina
Established August 1970
Sub.: U.S.: Individual:$8;Institution: $30
Distribution: Monthly
Circulation: U.S.:10,000
Spanish, English text
50% (approx)non-English
Freelance articles accepted

SASE for ms.return
Ms.lang.: No preference
Query, letter
No ms.length indicated
No payment
Photos/cr./no pay
Tabloid
Size: 10" x 16.5"
Black/white; 1 color
Newsprint paper
Paper color: Not listed
Display, classified
Deadline: Call for information
Outside readers: Unknown
No "kill" fee

El Tecolote Newspaper focuses on the issues and culture of

Chicanos and Latinos, with interests in other Third World cultures, such as the Philippines, Palestine and others.

The editor says the newspaper has a heavy emphasis on community issues and political questions at the national, international and regional levels which may affect the community. Some cultural reporting and analysis is included.

The editor's suggestions to contributors: "Know your technique; know your subject matter."

(Cross-referenced: Chicano.)

Latvian
MAZPUTNINS
Editor: Andra Zommers
100 Cherry Hill Drive
Kalamazoo
Michigan 49007
No telephone listing
Publisher: Latvian Institute
Established 1959
Subscription: U.S.:$24
Distribution: Monthly
Cir.: U.S.:500; Intl.:100
Latvian text
100% Latvian
Freelance articles accepted

SASE: Not indicated
Latvian ms.lang.prefer
Query: Not indicated
No ms.length indicated
No payment
Photos/credits/no pay
Magazine
Size: 8.5" x 11"
Black/white/color
Bond paper
White color paper
No advertising
Deadline: Not listed
No outside gp.readers
No "kill" fee

Mazputnins, a Latvian language magazine, is described as "striving to provide good Latvian literature to young children as well as information on Latvian heritage."

The editor had no suggestions for contributors.

Lithuanian
AIDAI/ECHOES/
Editor: L. Andriekus, O.F.M.
361 Highland Blvd.
Brooklyn
New York 11207
(718) 235-5962
Pub.: Lithuanian Franciscan Fathers
Established 1945
Subscription: U.S.:$20; Intl.:$20
Distribution: Quarterly
Circulation: U.S. & Intl.:1,300
Lithuanian text
100% non-English
Freelance articles accepted

SASE: Not required
No ms.lang.preferred
Query, letter
No ms.length indicated
Payment negotiated
Photos: Staff assigned
Format: Not listed
Size: 9" x 12"
Black/white
Paper type: Not listed
White color paper
No advertising
Deadline: Not listed
Outside group readers
No "kill" fee

AIDAI/Echoes covers religion, philosophy, literature and art.

Lithuanian
LITUANUAI
Editor: Lituanus Foundation
6621 So. Troy Street
Chicago
Illinois 60629
No telephone listing
Publisher: Lituanus Foundation
Established 1954
Subscription: U.S.:$10; Intl.:$15
Distribution: Quarterly
Circulation: U.S.:3,200; Intl.:500
English text
0% non-English
Freelance articles accepted

SASE: No response
English ms.preference
Query unnec.;letter O.K.
No ms.length indicated
No payment
Photos/credits/no pay
Format: Not listed
Size: Not listed
Black/white
Newsprint paper
White color paper
No advertising
Deadline: Not listed
Linguists, historians
No "kill" fee

Lituanuai readers are, according to the editor, interested in everything about Lithuania (Latvia and Estonia), with special interest in humanities, social sciences, etc.

The editor's advice to contributors is to "write well."

Lithuanian
MUSU ZINIOS/Our News
Editor: Rev.A. Saulaitis
5620 S. Claremont Ave.
Chicago
Illinois 60636
(312) 778-7500 or 737-8400
Pub.: Lithuanian Youth Ctr./Jesuit Fr.
Established 1968
Subscription: U.S. & International:$8
Distribution: Monthly since 1979
Cir.: U.S.:1,690; Intl.:10; Contl.:50
Lithuanian text
100% non-English
No freelance accepted

SASE: Not applicable
Lithuanian ms.preferred
Query, phone/letter
No ms.length indicated
No payment
Photos staff assigned
Tabloid
Size: 8.5" x 11"
Black/white
Regular paper
White color paper
Display ads
Deadline: 15th of month
No outside group readers
No "kill" fee

Musu Zinios (Our News) publishes articles about activities at the Youth Center and the Lithuanian Jesuit Fathers, primarily in the Chicago area. There are also articles about cultural, religious, social educational, artistic activies, and so forth, published in this periodical.

The editor describes the publication as addressing the religious and community concerns of Lithuanian Americans in the Chicago area.

The editor's tips for contributors: "Contributions are limited to those who actually participate in the activities and describe them or comment on them in articles and photographs."

This periodical is published in Lithuanian, and the publisher/editor translates the articles if necessary.

Musu Zinios is described as 20 pages long.

Lithuanian
TIESA
Editor's Name: Not listed
26 North Street; Room 42
Middletown
New York 10940
(914) 343-3774
Pub.: Assoc.of Lithuanian Workers
Established 1930
Subscription: Membership
Distribution: Monthly
Circulation controlled: U.S.: Members only
English text
0% non-English
Freelance not accepted/Staff assigned

SASE: Not applicable
English ms.preference
Query: Not applicable
No ms.length indicated
No pay articles
No photos
Newsletter
Size: Not listed
Black/white
Paper type: Unlisted
White color paper
No advertising
Deadline: Not listed
No outside group readers
"Kill" fee: Not applicable

Tiesa's editor says, "Our paper is only for our membership. Material all submitted by members."

The newsletter is sent to members of the Association only. (Author's Note: Although *Tiesa's* editorial representative returned a completed questionnaire, the publication's representative requested the publication not be included on mailing lists.)

M

Metis, American Indian
PAN-AMERICAN INDIAN ASSOCIATION NEWS
Editor: Chief Piercing Eyes
P.O. Box 244
Nocatee
Florida 33864
(813)494-6930
Publisher:Chief Piercing Eyes
Established January 1984
Subscription: U.S.:$12;Intl.:N/A
Distribution:Three to five times/yr.
Circulation: U.S.: 4,500; Intl.: 50
English text
0-1% non-English
Freelance articles accepted

SASE: Not required
English ms.preferred
Query unnecessary
Ms.lgth.: 1-2 pages
No payment
Photos/credits/no pay
Tabloid
Size: Not listed
Black/white
Newsprint paper
White color paper
Display ads
Deadline: Not listed
Anthro.,ecolog.,NewAge
No "kill" fee

Pan-American Indian Association News, formerly *The Tribal Advisor* seeks to help Indian and Metis recapture or discover their ancient heritage and apply it to a modern world, according to the editor. The publication puts a heavy emphasis on genealogy and its genetic and spiritural implications and revival groups, including how to start a revival group and so forth.

The editor, Chief Piercing Eyes, in describing the editorial content of the publication, writes, "(Publication) of a practical understanding of issues pertaining to the reviving Indian. We seek to correct misunderstanding of traditionalism, especially in revival groups. While the whole matter of genetic upsurge and returning to traditional values is taken in deadly seriousness, it is pursued in a lightly humorous vein without too much doomsday.

"If it isn't fun, it probably isn't worth doing.

"We try to avoid revenge and violence and emphasize 'getting even' through exposure and good humor. We don't want outsiders afraid of us or other revival groups," Chief Piercing Eyes writes of the publication.

For contributors, the editor comments, "Camera-ready copy in 5" columns ready to clip and paste greatly tempt us to use them. Send for a free sample copy to study. Nothing illegal. Violence only in historical sense. We want materials that emphasize displaced Reservation Indians 'getting along' in modern society without losing traditional identity (a tricky exercise), and we want revival Indians to gain a sense of destiny and avoid revenge fantasies. Don't take yourself too seriously. Let's enjoy reviving our heritage."

(Cross-referenced: American Indian.)

Mexican-American
COMEXAZ: NEWS MONITOR SERVICE
Editor: G. Mendoza
Old address:
Box 12062
Oakland, California 94604

The questionnaire unclaimed and no forwarding address was available.

Mohawk, Native American
AKWESASNE NOTES
Editor: D. George; M. Narsisian
P.O. Box 196; Mohawk Nation
Rooseveltown
New York 13683-0196
(518) 358-9531 or (518) 358-9535
Publisher: Mohawk Nation
Established 1968
Sub.: U.S.:$10/15;Intl.:$20/35(2nd/1stClass)
Distribution: Bimonthly
Circulation: U.S.:13,000; Intl.:2,000
English text
0% non-English
Freelance articles accepted

SASE: Required
English ms.prefer
Query, letter
No ms.length indicated
No payment
Photos
Tabloid
Size: 11.5" x 15"
Black/White
Newsprint paper
White color paper
No ads
Deadline: Unlisted
Envir.;Human Rights activists
No "kill" fee

Akwesasne Notes is published by the Mohawk Nation for indigenous peoples the world over, and it is the official publication of the Mohawk People of Akwesasne (New York-Canada border). The focus of the editorial content is the documentation and analysis of the worsening situation of indigenous peoples in the world.

They support the respect of basic human rights and the conscious application of human values to man-made technologies. Peace and harmony are among the issues supported by the group.

The philosophy of the newsletter is to publish information that is supportive and expresses the group's ideals.

(Cross-referenced: Native American.)

Muslim, Arab
ARAMCO WORLD
Editor: Robert Arndt
P.O. Box 4534
Houston
Texas 77210
(713) 432-4425
Publisher: Aramco
Established 1951
Sub.: U.S.:$0 (Controlled)
Distribution: Bimonthly
Cir.: U.S.:135,000; Intl.:30,000
English text
0% non-English
Freelance articles accepted

SASE: Not required
English ms.prefer
Query, letter
No ms.lgth.indicated
Payment
Photos/credits/pay
Magazine
Size: 8.5" x 11"
Black/white/color
Glossy paper
White color paper
No advertising
Deadline: Not listed
Journalists,libs.,others
Pays "kill" fee

Aramco World is described by the editor as providing coverage of the history, culture, geography and economics of the Arab and Muslim world.

This magazine is received by many libraries and is widely read by journalists and other persons interested in oil and the Middle East.

Freelance articles and ideas are used. Authors are paid a flat fee if their contributions are used by Aramco World. If the idea is used but not the article, the author is paid a "kill" fee. The amount of the fee is determined at the editor's discretion.

Freelance photos are used, credits and payment are given. The fee for use of freelance photos is determined by agreement with the photographer or on a space-rate basis.

The editor looks for a balance between writings from within the Middle East and from outside the area. Authors should keep in mind that the readership is open-minded, but not well-informed on the subject.

The editor writes, "If there is any 'gee-whiz,' it had better come from the subject, not from the writing."

(Cross referenced: Arab.)

N

Native American
AMERICAN INDIAN EDUCATION, JOURNAL OF
Editor: John Red Horse
413 Farmer Building
Arizona State University
Tempe, Arizona 85287
(602) 965-6292
Pub.: Center for Indian Education
Established June 1961
Subscription: U.S.:$14; International:$16.50
Distribution: Three times/year
Circulation: U.S./International Total:550
English text
0% non-English
Freelance articles accepted

SASE: No response
English ms.preferred
Query: No preference
No ms.length indicated
No payment
Photos: If needed
Journal
Size: 40 pages long
Black/white
Glossy paper
White color paper
Ads: No response
Deadline: Unlisted
Libraries
"Kill" fee: N/A

The *Journal of American Indian Education* publishes papers specifically related to the education of North American Indians and Alaskan Natives. The emphasis is on research in the experimental, historical and field study reports.

The manuscript requirements are extensive and clearly written. Authors who plan to submit a manuscript for consideration by the editor would benefit by obtaining a copy of the guidelines prior to submission of the manuscript.

Native American
CHEROKEE ADVOCATE
Editor: Mrs. Lynn Howard
P.O. Box 948
Tahlequah
Oklahoma 74465
(918) 456-0671
Pub.: Cherokee Nation of Oklahoma
Established 1977
Subscription: U.S.:$10; International:$20
Distribution: Monthly
Circulation: U.S.:4,995; International:5
English text
0% non-English
No freelance accepted/Staff assigned

SASE: Not applicable
English ms.preference
Query: Phone or letter
No ms.length indicated
No payment
No photos accepted
Tabloid
Size: No response
Black/white/color
Newsprint paper
White color paper
Display, classified
Deadline: 1st of month
Libs., museums, schools
No "kill" fee

Cherokee Advocate is described as having an Indian (Native American) ethnic-interest audience. It is the official publication of the

Cherokee Nation of Oklahoma. News of programs and services and administration issues are among the subjects covered in the publication.

As no freelance articles or photos are accepted, the editor provided no tips for contributors.

Native American
CHEROKEE BOYS CLUB NEWSLETTER
Editor: Stan Bienick
P.O. Box 507
Cherokee
North Carolina 28719
(704) 497-9101
Publisher: Cherokee Boys Club, Inc.
Established 1970
Subscription: Controlled (members)
Distribution: Quarterly
Circulation: U.S.:3,600
English text
0% non-English
No freelance accepted

SASE: Not applicable
English ms.preference
Query: Not applicable
Ms.length: Not applicable
No payment
Photos: Staff assigned
Newsletter
Size: Not listed
Print color: Not listed
Paper type: Not listed
Paper color: Not listed
No advertising
Deadline: Not applicable
Libraries
No "kill" fee

Cherokee Boys Club Newsletter is published for use by enrolled members of the Eastern Band of Cherokee Indians, donors and friends. The content is described by the editor as informative and inspirational.

The editor provided no tips for contributors.

Native American
CHEROKEE ONE FEATHER, THE
Editor: Richard L. Welch
P.O. Box 455
Cherokee
North Carolina 28719
(704) 497-5513
Pub.: Eastern Band Cherokee Indians
Established July 1967
Subscription: No information
Distribution: Weekly
Circulation: U.S.:2,000
English, Sequoyan syllabary (Cher.Lang.)
1% Cherokee (Sequoyan Syllabary)
Freelance articles accepted

SASE: No response
English ms.prefer
Query: Phone O.K.
No ms.length indicated
No payment
Photos/credits
Tabloid
Size: 13" x 9.75"
Black/white
Newsprint paper
Pap.color: Newsprint
Display, classified
Deadline: Monday noon
Outside group readers
No "kill" fee

The Cherokee One Feather publishes news of interest to the Native

American Community. The editorial content is further described as "For the common good and right of people to know. The periodical serves as a stimulus which generates interest with well-formed opinions, expressed clearly and forcefully with room for contrary opinions without arrogance or intolerance. The primary function of this periodical is to report the news."

The editor asks that freelance writers contact them for approval request before submitting articles.

Native American
DAYBREAK STAR INDIAN READER
Editor: Kathryn Oneita
1945 Yale Place East
Seattle
Washington 98102
(206) 325-0070
Pub.: United Indians of All Tribes Foundation
Established 1975
Sub.: U.S.:Sliding scale rates.Ask for info.
Distribution: Oct.-May, monthly
Circulation: 4,500
English text
0% non-English
Freelance accepted (See description)

SASE: Recommended
English ms.preferred
Query:Recommended
No ms.lgth.indicated
Pay: Certificate given
Photos: None
Magazine
Size: 8.5" x 10.75"
Black/white/one color
Newsprint paper
Newsprint color
No advertising
Deadline: Not listed
Some libraries receive
"Kill" fee: Not appl.

Daybreak Star Indian Reader, a 24-page children's learning resource, is co-produced by Indian students and an adult staff. The magazine is described as having a flexibility that permits students of differing abilities and interests to benefit from the articles and exercises.

Daybreak Star Indian Reader contains accurate articles that range from information about tribal traditions and legends to creative writing exercises, math and science activities and much more. The traditions of Native American cultural regions is reflected in a readership which extends from coast to coast. The content is culturally-focused with activities to interest all students in grades 4 to 6, although there are some subscribers in grades 7-12.

In the tenth annual report to the U.S. Congress, *Daybreak Star Indian Reader*, was named by the National Advisory Council on Indian Education as an exemplary program that receives funds under the Indian Education Act.

For contributors: "Students in classrooms around the country are encouraged to submit their writing and drawing projects for inclusion in monthly issues." Teachers should contact the editor prior to submitting freelance materials.

Native American
INDIAN AFFAIRS
Editor: Gelvin Stevenson
95 Madison Ave.
New York
New York 10016
(212) 689-8720
Pub.: Assoc.on Indian Affairs,Inc
Established 1923 circa.
Sub.: U.S.:$25 Member;$10 newsletter only
Distribution: Quarterly
Circulation: U.S.:25,000
English text
0% non-English
Freelance: No response

SASE: Suggested
English ms.prefer
Query: Required
No ms.length indicated
Pay: No information
Photos: Query first
Newsletter
Size: 8.5" x 11"
Black/white
Regular paper
White paper color
No advertising
Deadline: Unknown
Anyone interested
"Kill" fee: Unknown

Indian Affairs publishes information concerning the advocacy for Native Americans and Alaska Natives in education, economic and community development legal defense, child welfare, health and public education.

The editorial content emphasizes happenings of major significance in current Indian Affairs: Self-determination, legal defense, education, health resource utilization, family defense, and youth issues among other things.

The newsletter, *Indian Affairs*, is available without membership in the organization, Association on American Indian Affairs, Inc. The cost is $10 per year. Membership dues are $25 per year, and includes the newsletter. Back issues of the newsletter are available for $2.50 each.

For contributors to *Indian Affairs*, Dr. Idrian N. Resnick, executive director writes, "We encourage those of you who are researchers or writers, who have or are willing to develop material on these and other Native American issues to let us know about your work and ideas. We certainly welcome help in producing high quality relevant material for Indian Affairs."

The Association's legal status is nonprofit, 501(c)3 corporation, governed by a 19-member Board of Directors, of whom 12 are American Indians and Native Alaskans. Funding: 50% members and direct mail; 50% legacies.

Native American
INDIAN EDUCATOR
1945 Yale Place East
Seattle, Washington 98102

Indian Educator is no longer in publication.

Native American
INDIAN PROGRESS
Editor: Ora Lee Mayberry
1410 Corregidor Street
Greensboro
North Carolina 27406
(919) 275-4265
Publisher: Ora Lee Mayberry
Established 1869
Subscription: $0 (Free)
Distribution: Three times/year
Circulation: U.S.:2,500
English text
0% non-English
Freelance articles accepted

SASE: No response
English ms.preference
Query: No response
No ms.length indicated
No payment
Photos accepted
Tabloid
Size: 9.5" x 12"
Black/white
Glossy paper
White color paper
Ads: No response
Deadline: Unknown
No outside readers
"Kill" fee: Not listed

Indian Progress publishes news from Five Indian Centers, four in Oklahoma and one in Alabama. The editor describes the editorial content as "presenting the news as it is."

Freelance articles and photographs are accepted, but space is described as limited, so there is no promise submitted materials will be used. There is no payment for freelance articles.

Native American
INDIAN TRADER, THE
Editor: Bill Donovan
P.O. Box 1421
Gallup
New Mexico 87301
(505) 722-6694
Publisher: Martin Link
Established April 1970
Sub.: U.S.:$15; Intl.:$26 (Controlled)
Distribution: Monthly
Cir.: U.S.:3,240;Intl.:250; Controlled:240
English text
0% non-English
Freelance articles accepted

SASE: Required
English ms.preference
Query necessary: Phone
No ms.length indicated
Payment, flat fee
Photos: Staff assigned
Tabloid
Size: 10" x 13"
Black/white print
Newsprint paper
White color paper
Display, classified
Deadline.: 1st of mo.b.pub.
Libraries subscribe
No "kill" fee paid

The editor of *The Indian Trader* describes the ethnic interests of the periodical as focused on "either arts and crafts dealers, collectors or persons interested in Indian culture or Old West history.

The editorial content is devoted to 80% Indian culture and art history and the remaining 20% devoted to Old West information.

The editor had no tips for contributors.

Native American
NARF LEGAL REVIEW
Editor: Susan Arkeketa
1506 Broadway
Boulder
Colorado 80303
(303) 447-8760
Pub.: Native American Rights Fund
Established 1972
Subscription: U.S./Intl.:Not given
Distribution: Quarterly
Circulation: U.S.and Intl. 22,000
English text
0% non-English
No freelance accepted/Staff

SASE: No response
English ms.preferred
No query
No ms.length indicted
No payment
No photos
Magazine
Size: 8.5" x 11"
Black/white
Paper type: Regular
White color paper
No advertising
Deadline: Not listed
Diverse audience
No "kill" fee

NARF Legal Review publishes articles which deal with Indian law issues.

The editor indicates that the readership is a diverse audience, and, since no freelance articles are accepted, there are no tips for contributors.

Native American
NATIVE NEVADAN, THE
Editor: Penny K. Russell-Roberts
98 Colony Road
Reno
Nevada 89502
(702) 329-2936
Publisher: Reno-Sparks Indian Colony
Established 1963
Subscription: U.S.:$12; International:$22
Distribution: Monthly
Circulation: U.S.:4,500; International:7
English text
0% non-English
Freelance articles accepted

SASE: Required
English ms.preference
Query unnecessary
No ms.length indicated
No payment
Photos accepted
Magazine
Size: 8" x 11"
Black/white/color
Newsprint paper
White color paper
Display, classified
Deadline: 3rd.Mon.ea.mo.
Govt., schools, libs.
"Kill" fee: No response

The Native Nevadan is described as a periodical with a primarily Native American readership, but non-ethnic-interest readers include government agencies, schools, libraries and social service agencies, and so forth.

According to the editor, *The Native Nevadan* publishes local, state and national news that involves Indian country. Additionally, feature articles, sports stories, and a history column are part of the editorial content.

The editor of *The Native Nevadan* did not provide any tips for contributors.

Native American
NISHNAWBE NEWS
No longer published.
Please refer to *Win Awenen Nisitotung*, Appendix A.

Native American
OHOYO
Ohoyo Resource Center; Ste.214
Old address:
2301 Midwestern Parkway
Witchita Falls, Texas 76308

The questionnaire was unclaimed and no forwarding address was available.

Native American
SEMINOLE TRIBUNE
Editor: Barbara Billie
6333 N.W. 30th St.
Hollywood
Florida 33024
(305) 583-7112, Ext.346
Pub.: Kim's Graphics/Tribal Council
Established October 1983
Subscription: U.S.:$15
Distribution: Biweekly
Circulation: U.S.:3,000 (Total)
English, Seminole text
% non-English: Minimal
Freelance articles accepted

SASE: No response
English ms.prefer
Query: Phone or letter
No ms.length indicated
Payment: Flat fee
Photos/credits/no pay
Newspaper
Size: 13.25" x 22"
Black/white/color
Newsprint paper
White color paper
Display, classified
Deadline: Not listed
Outside group readers
No "kill" fee

The readership of *The Seminole Tribune* is described as Native American.

The editor says, "(Articles) must be Indian-related topics or health related. Indian poetry and artwork requested and welcomed."

English is used in the publication along with some Seminole (Miccosukee and Creek), but these languages are, according to the editor, only used once in a while.

Native American
SENTINEL/BULLETIN-NCAI NEWS
Editor: Suzan Shown Harjo
804 D St. N.E.
Washington
D.C. 20002
(202) 546-9404
Pub.: National Congress American Indians
Est.: U.S.:1944; NCAI News: 1985
Subscription: U.S.:$10
Distribution: Bimonthly (approx)
Circulation:U.S.: 2,500; Intl.:0
English text
0% non-English
No freelance articles accepted

SASE: Not applicable
English ms.preference
Query: Telephone
No ms.length indicated
No payment
No photos accepted
Magazine
Size: Not listed
Black/white/color
Paper type: Regular
White color paper
Ads: No response
Deadline: Not listed
Outside group readers
No "kill" fee

Sentinel/Bulletin readership is interested in the issues and concerns of Indian and Native governments and individuals. According to the editor, the editorial contents are set by the policy statements and goals of the organization, National Congress of American Indians, and the membership.

According to the editor, this periodical is an organizational publication that publishes articles from a wide array of topics of interest to the membership. Friends of the organization have collaborated on articles, but are not paid for doing so.

Native American
TURTLE QUARTERLY MAGAZINE
Editor: Tim Johnson
25 Rainbow Mall
Niagara Falls
New York 14303
(716) 284-2427
Pub.: Native American Center
Established December 30, 1986
Sub.: U.S.:$10; Intl.:$12
Distribution: Quarterly
Cir.: U.S.:1,500; International:500
English text
0% non-English
Freelance articles accepted

SASE: Required
English manuscript prefer
Query unnec.; call/write ed.
No ms.length indicated
Pay by length and research
Photos/credits/payment
Magazine
Size: Not listed
Black/white/color
Glossy paper
White color paper
Display
Deadline: Not listed
Coll.,libs.,univ.,others
"Kill" fee: No response

Turtle Quarterly Magazine publishes material about Native American art, culture, history, contemporary issues and the environment. Among the non-ethnic group subscribers are colleges, libraries, universities and others interested in Native American culture.

The editor's comments to contributors: "Don't be afraid to suggest ideas, write or call. We need contributors."

Native American
WICAXO SA REVIEW
Editor: Elizabeth Cook-Lynn
MS 188; Eastern Wash.Univ.
Cheney
Washington 99004
(509) 359-2871
Pub.: Indian Studies Dept./English
Established 1985
Sub.: U.S.:$8-15; Intl.:Unknown
Distribution: Biannual
Circulation: U.S.:210; Intl.:15
English text, some translations
1% non-English
Freelance articles accepted

SASE: Required
English ms.preference
Query unnecessary
Ms.lgth.max.: 6-8,000 wds.
No pay, copies given
Photos/credits/no pay
Magazine
Size: Not listed
Black/white
Glossy paper
White color paper
Display
Deadline: Not listed
Pub/Univ.libs.,individuals
No "kill" fee

"*Wicaxo Sa Review* is," according to the editor, "devoted to the development of Native American Studies as an academic discipline. We are interested in receiving short manuscripts (see maximum length of manuscripts listed above) of scholarly articles and essays, poems, short stories, book reviews, literary criticism, critiques of texts, course outlines, syllabi, curriculum designs, pedagogical technique discussions and teacher apparatuses useful to the development of the discipline. We wish to serve as a publishing outlet and as a resource for Native American scholars and readers."

For prospective contributors, the editor writes, "We are *not* eclectic, but we are *open-minded*. Each issue will contain several articles, three poems, one short story or narrative, four short book reviews or critiques of texts and one 'profile' of a Native American scholar who has made a significant contribution to the discipline."

Native American
WILDFIRE
Editor: Matt Ryan
P.O.Box 9167
Spokane
Washington 99201
(509) 326-6561
Publisher: Bear Tribe Medicine Society
Established 1984
Subscription: U.S.:$5; International:$10
Distribution: Quarterly
Cir.: U.S.:7,000; Intl.:1,000
English text
0% non-English
Freelance articles accepted

SASE: Required
English ms.preference
Query unnecessary
No ms.length indicated
Payment, flat fee
Photos/credits/pay
Magazine
Size: Not listed
Black/white/color
Paper: Electrobrite
White color paper
Display, classified
Deadline: May 30; Nov.30
Libs., community schools
No "kill" fee

Wildfire has a Native American readership focus, and the editor also writes, "New Age" perspective, ecology, sexuality, earth awareness, individual growth-healing and responsibility are areas of interest to the readers.

The editorial content is described as "interested in any life-positive material from any perspective that embraces a feeling of life, i.e., people, animals, plants and earth as the central issue, and other articles that seek to promote, protect and increase the value of life processes."

The editors encourage contributors to read *Wildfire* and get a sense of what the publication is about. The accentuation and interpretation of the facts are important to the editor who also writes, "Avoid cynicism, slickness and cuteness. Do not avoid HARD truths, but accent the positive. We do not accept complaining defeatism."

Native American
WOTANIN WOWAPI
Editor: Minnie Two Shoes
P.O. Box 493
Poplar
Montana 59255
(406) 768-5155, Ext.369 or 370
Pub.: Ft.Peck Assiniboine/Sioux Tribe
Established 1969
Subscription: Not listed
Distribution: Weekly
Circulation: U.S.:1,700 (Total)
English text
0% non-English
Freelance articles accepted

SASE: Required
English ms.preference
Query: Phone, letter
No ms.length indicated
Pay/flat fee/by word
Photos/credits/pay
Newspaper
Size: 13" x 21"
B/W; color.spec.editions
Newsprint paper
White color paper
Display, classified
Deadline:Tues.,4:30 p.m.
Oil co.,local TV, radio
No "kill" fee

Wotanin Wowapi ethnic interests are described, by the editor, as diverse.

"We have both Christian and traditional Native American readers from both on and off the reservation," writes the editor.

"We try hard to have editorials in two or three issues in a month. We like national and regional news, but not too much. We're trying to get better sports coverage and school activity coverage."

The editor, Minnie Two Shoes, says, "I'm always looking for human interest stories on Native Americans, preferably our tribal members. I'm interested also in solutions to problems or unique programs or ideas that other tribes share."

Native American
YAKIMA NATION REVIEW
Editor: Ronn L. Washines
P.O. Box 386
Toppenish
Washington 98948-0386
(509) 865-5121
Publisher: Yakima Indian Nation
Established May 1970
Sub.: U.S.:$15; International:None listed
Distribution: Bimonthly
Cir.: U.S.:2,500 (Total)
English text
0% to minimal non-English
Freelance articles accepted

SASE: Required
English ms.preference
Query: No preference
No ms.length indicated
Payment
Photos/credits/no pay
Newspaper
Size: Standard
Black/white
Newsprint paper
White color paper
Display, classified
Deadline: 72 hrs.bef.pub.
Libs., govt.agencies
No "kill" fee

Yakima Nation Review publishes information about the Yakima

Nation, and from time to time, articles of interest to the Indian tribes and the non-Indian ethnic groups are published.

Yakima Nation Review publishes articles relative to the overall concern for the preservation of the Yakima Indian Nation, its people, resources and culture according to the description provided by the editor.

For writers who submit articles to Yakima Nation Review, the editor writes, "Tie in, locally or regionally, with specific ethnic target readership. Be prepared to substantiate the authenticity of information regarding any historical, cultural or geographical data included."

Native American, American Indian	SASE: Not indicated
AMER.INDIAN CULTURE AND RESEARCH JOUR.	English ms.prefer
Editor: Hanay Geigomah	Query unnec./ltr.o.k.
3220 Campbell Hall	No ms.lgth.indicated
Univ.of California Los Angeles	No pay for articles
Los Angeles, California 90024-1548	No photos/cr./no pay
(213) 825-4777	Magazine
Pub.: American Indian Studies Center	Size: 130 page lgth.
Established 1976	Black/white
Sub.: U.S:$20/yr; International:$21/yr	Glossy paper
Distribution: Quarterly	White color paper
Circulation: U.S.:650; Intl.:50	Display
English text	Deadline: Not listed
0% non-English	Hist.,myth.profs.
Freelance articles accepted	No "kill" fee

This journal, *American Indian Culture and Research Journal* is written for people interested in any significant research or topic about Native Americans and/or for those who have concerns regarding American Indians.

Outside group readers include anthropologists, English or literature professors, policy-makers and lawyers in addition to the above listing.

Papers submitted to the journal are "blind-refereed papers by three or more referees. The editors invite comments on scholarly and policy issues, but the editorial staff does not write editorials."

The editors suggest contributors follow the guidelines in the journal for submission of articles.

(Cross-reference: American Indian.)

Native American, American Indian
AMERICAN INDIAN LAW NEWSLETTER
Editor: Marc Mannes
P.O. Box 4456; Station A
Albuquerque
New Mexico 87196
(505) 277-5462
Pub.: American Indian Law Center,Inc.
Established 1968
Sub.: U.S.:$15 (Am.Ind.); $20 (gen.pub.)
Distribution: Bimonthly
Circulation: U.S.:600; International:100
English text
0% non-English
Freelance articles accepted

SASE: Required
English ms.prefer
Query, letter
No ms.length indicated
No payment
No photos
Magazine
Size: 8.5" x 11"
Black/white
Regular paper
Cream color paper
Ads: No information
Deadline: Unlisted
Libs.,govt., others
No "kill" fee

American Indian Law Newsletter publishes articles concerning American Indian Law and related subjects.

With respect to tips to contributors, the editor writes, "We use only articles dealing with current issues or topics concerning American Indian Law."

The editors do not use freelance ideas.

Native American, American Indian
INDIAN CRUSADER
Editor: Basil M. Gaynor
4009 S.Halldale Ave.
Los Angeles
California 90062-1851
(213) 299-1810
Pub.: Am.Indian Liber.Crusade,Inc.
Established 1952
Subscription: U.S.:Donation
Distribution: Quarterly
Circulation: U.S.:4,026; International:6
English text
0% non-English
No freelance articles accepted

SASE: Not applicable
English ms.preference
Query: No response
No ms.length indicated
No payment
No photos accepted
Newspaper
Size: 8.5" x 11"
Black/white
Glossy paper
White color paper
Ads: No information
Deadline: Not listed
Radio broadcast listeners
"Kill" fee: No response

Indian Crusader publishes articles about American Indians, but the editor says the readers are nearly all "Anglo."

Many of the subscribers are people who listen to the radio broadcasts, and in turn, the listeners send in a donation and a request to be put on the mailing lists.

According to the editor, "We try to portray the condition of the

Indians on the reservations of the United States, particularly in the Southwest and in North Carolina."

No suggestions for contributors were provided.

Native American, American Indian
WHISPERING WIND MAGAZINE
Editor: Jack B. Heriard
8009 Wales St.
New Orleans
Louisiana 70126-1952
(504) 241-5866
Pub.: Louisiana Indian Herit.Assoc.,Inc.
Established October 1967
Sub.: U.S.:$12; Intl.:$14
Distribution: Bimonthly
Cir.: U.S.:3,875; International:125
English text
0% non-English
Freelance articles accepted

SASE: Required
English ms.preference
Query unnecessary
No ms.length indicated
Pay in copies only
Photos accepted
Magazine
Size: 8.5" x 11"
Black/white
Glossy paper
White color paper
Display, classified
Deadline: 60 da.before pub.
Lib.,prisons,N.A.enthusiasts
No "kill" fee

According to the editor of *Whispering Wind Magazine*, 59 percent of the readers are American Indian. Among the non-ethnic interest readers, the editor lists libraries, prisons, youth groups, American Indian enthusiasts who have a sincere interest in the American Indian, but who are not American Indian, as magazine subscribers.

The magazine contains articles about American Indian crafts and material culture, past and present. Historical manuscripts relating to the American Indian are published and the magazine is fully illustrated.

The editor's tips for contributors, are as follows:

"Articles should be submitted typed, double-spaced and in duplicate. One set of photos, if necessary for the article, should accompany the manuscript.

"Illustrations can be rough; the writer need not be an artist. The magazine maintains an artist on staff.

"Articles that are of historical content or make reference to previously published accounts should have a complete bibliography.

"New authors (not previously published extensively) are given some preference and encouragement to submit to *Whispering Wind.*"

Native American, Amer.Ind., Alaska Nat.
NATIVE PRESS RESEARCH JOURNAL
Eds.:Daniel F. Littlefield; J.W. Parins
502 Stabler Hall; U of Arkansas-Little Rock
Little Rock
Arkansas 72204
(501) 569-3160
Pub.: American Native Press Archives
Established Spring 1986
Sub.: U.S.,Intl.,Inst.:$12; Free:N.A.
Distribution: Quarterly
Circulation: U.S.:745; Intl.:5
English text
0% non-English
Freelance articles accepted

SASE: Not required
English ms.preferred
Query unnecessary
No ms.length indicated
No payment
No photos
Magazine
Size: Not listed
Black/white
Heavy bond paper
White color paper
No ads
Deadline: Unlisted
Acad.,St.,Pub.libraries
No "kill" fee

Native Press Research Journal publishes scholarly articles on American Native publishing, journalism, journalists, etc., as well as profiles of current or historical American Indian and Alaska Native periodicals.

This periodical is free to Native American and Alaska Native tribal groups. Outside groups which subscribe and receive the journal are academic, state and public libraries.

The editors say that no editorials are published and that views expressed in the academic articles do not necessarily reflect the views of the editors.

The editors further say the publisher of the journal is a "poor" academic department, thus no payments can be given to contributors whose articles are published.

With respect to suggestions for prospective contributors, the editors write, "Get a copy of the first issue and see what our publishing goals are; then look at subsequent issues to see the kinds of topics we publish.

"Success depends on aiming at our audience as it does in any kind of writing. We seek well-researched articles or authoritatively-written articles by those who have been involved in the native press."

(Cross-referenced: American Indian, Alaska Natives.)

Native Amer.,Ethnic Stud.,Asian-Am.,Black,Hispanic	SASE: Required
EQUAL OPPORTUNITY MAGAZINE	English ms.prefer
Editor: James Schneider	Query, letter
44 Broadway	No ms.length
Greenlawn	Pay by word
New York 11740	Photos/credits/pay
(516) 261-8917	Magazine
Pub.: Equal Opportunity Pub.,Inc.	Size: 8" x 10"
Established 1969	B/W, Color
Subscription: U.S.:$13/yr.	Glossy paper
Distribution: Three times/yr.	White paper
Circulation: U.S.:15,000 (Controlled)	Display, classified
English text	Deadline: 6 wk.pr.
0% non-English	Coll.administrators
Freelance articles accepted	"Kill" fee: Unknown

The editor says about *Equal Opportunity Magazine*: "Our magazine is received by college students and young professionals who are Black, Hispanic, Native American and Asian-American. The focus is on career-guidance and job information."

This magazine provides role-model profiles, career-guidance topics and news of career opportunities for minorities.

The editors encourage writers to target articles specifically for the audience just described. Writers should present well-written, clean and professional manuscripts. Please include cover letter which details writing experience.

Those who wish to place either display or classified ads must submit the ad materials six weeks prior to desired publication date.

(Cross-referenced: Asian-American, Black, Ethnic studies, Hispanic.)

Native American, Mohawk
AKWESASNE NOTES
Editor: D. George; M. Narsisian
P.O. Box 196; Mohawk Nation
Rooseveltown
New York 13683-0196
(518) 358-9531 or (518) 358-9535
Publisher: Mohawk Nation
Established 1968
Sub.: U.S.:$10/15;Intl.:$20/35(2nd/1st.Cl.)
Distribution: Bimonthly
Circulation: U.S.:13,000; Intl.:2,000
English text
0% non-English
Freelance articles accepted

SASE: Required
English ms.preferred
Query, letter
No ms.length indicated
No payment
Photos
Tabloid
Size: 11.5" x 15"
Black/White
Newsprint paper
White color paper
No ads
Deadline: Unlisted
Envir.; Human Rights activists
No "kill" fee

Akwesasne Notes is published by the Mohawk Nation for indigenous peoples the world over, and it is the official publication of the Mohawk People of Akwesasne (New York-Canada border). The focus of the editorial content is the documentation and analysis of the worsening situation of indigenous peoples in the world.

They support the respect of basic human rights and the conscious application of human values to man-made technologies. Peace and harmony are among the issues supported by the group.

The philosophy of the newsletter is to publish information that is supportive and expresses the group's ideals.

(Cross-referenced: Mohawk.)

Norwegian
NEWS OF NORWAY
Editor: Mr. Bjarne Flolo
2720-34th Street,N.W.
Washington
D.C. 20008
(202) 333-6000
Pub.: Royal Norwegian Embassy
Established 1941
Subscription: U.S.:0; International:0
Distribution: Monthly
Cir.: U.S.:12,000; Intl.:1,000
English text
0% non-English
Freelance articles accepted

SASE: No response
English manuscript prefer
Query: No response
No ms.length indicated
No payment
Photos/cr.if req.; no pay
Newspaper
Size: 8.5" x 11"
Black/white/color
Newsprint paper
Off-white color paper
Ads: No response
Deadline: Not listed
Libs.,govt.,univ.; US comp.
No "kill" fee

News of Norway brings news and information on current economic, political and cultural events in Norway to its readers.

The editor describes the editorial content of the periodical as a governmental paper which focuses on facts and objective information plus debate.

The editor says that contributor's articles of interest to the publication must focus on Norwegian-American relations, culture and so forth.

Norwegian	SASE: Not required
WESTERN VIKING (WASHINGTON POSTEN)	No ms.lang.prefer
Editor: Henning C. Boe	Query unnecessary
2040 N.W. Market St.; Box 70408	No ms.length indicated
Seattle	No pay for freelance
Washington 98107	Photos/credits only
(206) 784-4617	Tabloid
Publisher: Western Viking Inc.	Size: Not listed
Established May 17, 1889	Black/white/color
Subscription: U.S.:$23; International:$24	Newsprint paper
Distribution: Weekly	White color paper
Circulation: U.S.:4,500; International:500	Display, classified
Norwegian, English text	Deadline: Fridays
65% non-English	No outside group readers
Freelance articles accepted	No "kill" fee

Western Viking publishes information to promote goodwill mostly between Norway and the USA. The articles are non-political and enlighten Norwegian-Americans about new developments in Norway and so forth.

The editor specifies that articles related to Norway and/or Norwegian-Americans are preferred, and sometimes general interest with respect to Scandinavians.

P

Polish
GLOS POLEK
Editor (English):Deiphine Lytell
205 S. Northwest Highway
Park Ridge
Illinois 60068
(312) 692-2247
Pub.: Polish Women's Alliance of Amer.
Established 1910
Subscription: U.S.: Controlled
Distribution: Bimonthly
Circulation: U.S.:24,500; Intl.:0
Polish, English text
75% non-English
Freelance articles accepted

SASE: No response
No ms.lang.preference
Query: No preference
No ms.length indicated
No pay/royalties/credits
Photos: Staff assigned
Newspaper
Size: 11" x 17" Approximate
Black/white, color ink
Newsprint paper
White color paper
No ads
Deadline: Not listed
No outside group readers
No "kill" fee

Glos Polek appeals to those people interested in the activities of the organization, Polish Women's Alliance of America. Polish ethnic news and features are also published.

With respect to the editorial content, the editor writes, "We aim to satisfy first, our organizational needs and then our leisure or social or political interests. The basic idea is that the Polish heritage is our main interest."

The editor further explains that no royalties are paid and the publication holds no copyrights.(Explanation of Col.2, line 4 above).

To the prospective freelance contributor, the editor writes,"If you don't want to be paid, send it to us. Maybe we'll use it."

Polish
POLISH AMERICAN JOURNAL
Editor: Larry Wroblewski
774 Fillmore Avenue
Buffalo
New York 14212
(716) 852-8211
Publisher: Panagraphics Corporation
Established October 1911
Sub.: U.S.:$10/yr; Intl.:$16/yr.
Distribution: Monthly
Cir.: Contl.: 20,000; Sub.:13,000
English, some Polish text
2-3% non-English
Freelance articles accepted

SASE: Not required
No ms.lang.preference
Query not necessary
No ms.length indicated
No payment
Photos/credits/no pay
Tabloid
Size: Not listed
Black/white/color
Newsprint paper
White color paper
Display, classified
Deadline: 20th of mo.b.pub.
Univ.,public libraries
No "kill" fee

The *Polish American Journal* publishes articles about current events, sports, opinions, tradition and history. The editorial content is described by the editor as activist, and encourages readers to pursue roots and feel secure in one's ethnicity. This publication is described by the editor as one which promotes dialogue between differing parties.

The editor suggests that contributors write stories with a national appeal; regional stories are used only if they have a national impact on the Polish American community.

Polish
POLISH HERITAGE
Editor: Wallace M. West
6520 - 109th Terrace North
Pinellas Park
Florida 33565
(813) 541-7875
Pub.: Amer.Council Polish Cult.Clubs
Established 1950
Subscription: U.S.:$6; Intl.:$7
Distribution: Quarterly
Circulation: U.S.:4,400; Intl.:100
English text
0% non-English
Freelance articles accepted

SASE: Not required
English ms.prefer
Query: No preference
No ms.lgth.indicated
No payment
Photos/credits/no pay
Newspaper
Size: 9" x 12"
Black/white
Glossy paper used
White color paper
No advertising
Deadline: Not listed
Univ.,pub.libraries
No "kill" fee

Polish Heritage, as described by the editor, emphasizes the history and culture of Poland. The primary aim of the periodical is to spread the knowledge of Poland's thousand year-old culture among Americans of all backgrounds and to enrich the evolving pattern of America's great culture by weaving into it the best from Polish sources of inspiration and accomplishment.

This periodical, as described by the editor, deals primarily with the intent and purpose of the American Council of Polish Cultural Clubs, and to inspire affiliate member organizations to promote cultural activities in their respective communities.

The editor prefers "articles that have relevance to Polish history and/or culture."

Polish
POLISH STUDIES NEWSLETTER
Editor: Albin S. Woznick
3433 Gregg Road
Brookeville
Maryland 20833
(301) 774-4560
Publisher: Albin S. Woznick
Established July 1979
Subscription: U.S.:$12; Intl.:$12
Distribution: Monthly
Circulation: U.S.:400; Intl.:50
English, some Pol.,Ger.,.Russ.,Fr.
% non-English: Minimal
Freelance articles accepted

SASE: Not required
Prefer other lang.ms.
Query,unnec.;phone O.K.
No ms.length indicated
No pay
No photos accepted
Newsletter
Size: 8.5" x 11"
Black/white print
Paper type: Not listed
Paper color: Not listed
Classified
Deadline: 15th of month
Libs.,parochial schools
No "kill" fee

Polish Studies Newsletter disseminates information of Polish affairs publications. The *Newsletter* contains evaluations of Polish affairs publications, mostly book and recent periodical literature.

The editor, Albin Woznick, indicated a preference for manuscripts in languages other than English, but no specific language was listed.

If writers wish to submit manuscripts for consideration, the editor writes that writers be well-versed in Polish affairs.

(Author's note: Contributors who plan to use a language other than English would benefit by checking with the editor before sending the manuscript.)

Polish
PROMIEN
Old address:
Polish National Alliance
Sports Youth Commission
6100 N. Cicero Ave.
Chicago, Illinois 60646

Ceased publication in 1982.

Polish-American
KOSCIUSZKO FOUNDATION NEWSLETTER, THE
Editorial Contact: Krystyna S. Olszer
15 East 65th Street
New York
New York 10021
(212) 734-2130
Pub.: The Kosciuszko Foundation
Established 1946
Subscription: No information
Distribution: Quarterly
Circulation: No information
English text
0% non-English
No freelance accepted/Staff assigned

SASE: No response
English ms.prefer
Query, letter
No ms.lgth.indicated
Pay: No information
Photos: Staff asgn.
Magazine
Size: 8.5" x 11"
Black/white
Paper type: Unlisted
White; No.60 paper
Ads: No information
Deadline: Not listed
No outside readers
No "kill" fee

The Kosciuszko Foundation Newsletter is published for Polish-Americans who are members of The Kosciuszko Foundation.

The Newsletter publishes information about the activities of Board members and Trustees, development of the Foundation's major programs, grants and scholarly exchange with Poland, news from regional chapters, cultural events at the K.F. House and contributions to the Kosciuszko Foundation funds.

No freelance articles are accepted.

Polish-American
NOROD POLSKI
Editor: Andrew Azarjew
984 Milwaukee Avenue
Chicago
Illinois 60622
(312) 278-9744
Pub.: Polish Roman Catholic Union
Established 1886
Subscription: No information
Distribution: Bimonthly
Circulation: U.S.: Controlled
Polish, English text
33% non-English
Freelance articles accepted

SASE: Required
No ms.lang.preference
Query: No prefer;letter O.K.
Ms.lgth.:2-3pp.Double-spaced
No payment
Photos accepted; credits
Tabloid
Size: Not listed
Black/white/color
Paper type: Not listed
White color paper
Ads: No response
Deadline: Not listed
No outside group readers
No "kill" fee

Norod Polski deals with all ethnic (groups), but Polish-American matters receive preference. In the periodical, eight pages are published in English and four in Polish.

The content is mostly fraternal, cultural and social.

If a writer wishes to contribute, the editor says stories should be no longer than 2-3 pages, double-spaced.

Polish-American
POLISH AMERICAN STUDIES
Editor: James S. Pula
984 Milwaukee Avenue
Chicago
Illinois 60622
(607) 777-6723 (Ed. offices)
Pub.: Polish American Hist.Association
Established 1944
Sub.:U.S.:$15;Intl.:$15;Inst.:$25
Distribution: Twice yearly
Circulation: U.S./International: 750
English text
0% non-English
Freelance articles accepted

SASE: Not required
English ms. preference
Query: No preference
No ms.length indicated
Pay: Not applicable
Photos/credits/no pay
Magazine
Size: 5.5" x 8"
Black/white
Paper type: Bond
White paper color
Display
Deadline: Not listed
Libs.,hist.soc.,soc.historians
"Kill" fee: Not applicable

Polish American Studies is a scholarly journal which contains articles, reviews and other information on Poles in the Western hemisphere. The editor of this journal describes the non-ethnic-interest readers as libraries, historical associations, immigration and social historians.

The editor writes, "We accept materials of a scholarly nature in all of the humanities and social sciences dealing with the Polish experience in the Americas and its European antecedents."

Contributors need to be aware that articles must be scholarly in nature.

Polish-American
POST EAGLE, THE
Editor: Chester Grabowski
800 Van Houten Ave.; P.O.Box 2127
Clifton
New Jersey 07015
(201) 473-5414
Pub.: Post Publishing Co.,Inc.
Established 1962
Sub.: U.S.:$15; Intl.:$25
Distribution: Weekly
Cir.: U.S.:16,400; International:100
English, sometimes Polish text
% non-English: Minimal
Freelance articles accepted

SASE: No response
English ms.preference
Query: No response
No ms.length indicated
No payment
Photos/credits/no pay
Tabloid
Size: 10" x 14"
Black/white
Newsprint paper
White color paper
Display, classified
Deadline:Wed.before Wed.pub.
Some outside group readers
No "kill" fee

The Post Eagle serves the interest of the Polish-American readership and focuses on direct news from Poland, Polish history, politics, news and social events, health, sports, arts and leisure.

The newspaper's circulation is listed in the press kit as 16,000 paid subscribers, representative of 300,000 readers in over 40 states and 5 countries.

The readership spans age groups from grade school children to senior citizens, and includes members of fraternal, social and veterans groups, political figures, entertainers, members of mixed marriages and so forth.

Most noticeable in the newspaper are the numerous photographs, all well-identified and described, covering a wide range of events.

The press kit information states: "We welcome any and all news items pertinent to our readers." The press kit is a plus with respect to information for contributors and advertisers alike.

Polish-American
ZGODA
Editor: W.A. Wierzewski
6100 N. Cicero Ave.
Chicago
Illinois 60646
(312) 286-0500, ext. 44
Pub.: Polish Natl.Alliance of N.A.
Established 1881
Subscription: U.S.:Free
Distribution: Bimonthly
Circulation: U.S.:96,000
Polish, English text
30%-50% non-English
Freelance art.acc./most staff asgn.

SASE: No response
No ms.lang.preference
Query, letter
No ms.length indicated
No pay or honorariums
Photos/credits; staff assigned
Magazine
Size: 14.5" x 11.5"
Black/white
Newsprint paper
White color paper
No ads
Deadline: Not listed
Institutions
No "kill" fee

Zgoda is described by the editor as the oldest and the most popular ethnic and fraternal magazine serving 300,000 Polish American from New England to California. The magazine serves the members of Polish National Alliance and publishes information about fraternal, cultural, sports and general news.

Additionally, there are sections which pertain to news from Poland, history and heritage, Polish history, culture and heritage, official matters, reports, statistics, medical advice, a Polish Chef, insurance, and photo stories on Polish-American activities.

With respect to tips for contributors, the editor says, "Zgoda is interested in any kind of the material covering the activities, achievements and problems of the Polish-Americans in the U.S. and in Poland."

Portuguese
JORNAL PORTUGUES(PORTUGUESE JOURNAL)
Editor: Alberto S. Lemos
1912 Church Lane
San Pablo
California 94806
(415) 237-0888
Publisher: Alberto Santos Lemos
Established August 1888
Subscription: U.S.:$15; International:Unknown
Distribution: Weekly
Circulation: U.S.:4,500; International:500
Portuguese, English text
90% non-English
Freelance articles accepted

SASE: No response
Portuguese ms.prefer
Query, letter
No ms.lgth.indicated
No payment
Photos/crs./no pay
Newspaper
Size: Not listed
Black/white
Newsprint paper
White color paper
Display
Deadline: Mondays
Unk.outside groups
No "kill" fee

Jornal Portugues is written and published for people who are interested in Portuguese culture and language.

The editor says the editorial content is aimed at encouraging the maintenance and learning of the Portuguese language, culture and traditions.

"(The paper) promotes and informs the comprehensive and large Portuguese community and keeps cultural, political and friendly ties and relations among people of Portugal, Brazil and USA," the editor writes in the questionnaire

The editor says historical articles about the USA, Portugal, Brazil and ex-Portuguese-African and Oriental possessions, news and information about civic and political events and comments, tourism, travel, art, music, especially Brazilian and Portuguese, folklore, space, life and science are published. The editor prefers space, life and science articles which are "not too technical."

Portuguese
PORTUGUESE TIMES
Editor: Manuel A. Ferreira
1709 Acushnet Ave; PO Box N-1288
New Bedford
Massachusetts 0246
(617) 997-3118
Publisher: Manuel A. Ferreira
Established February 8, 1971
Sub.: U.S.:$15; International:$120 (Air Mail)
Distribution: Weekly
Circulation: U.S.:10,800; Intl.:200
Portuguese text
99% non-English
Freelance articles accepted

SASE: Not required
No ms.lang.prefer
Query OK; letter
No ms.length indic.
Pay/fl.fee; by feature
Photos/credits/no pay
Tabloid
Size: Not listed
Black/white/color
Newsprint paper
White color paper
Display, classified
Deadline: Monday
Univ.,cultural institutions
Pays "kill" fee

Portuguese Times publishes news from Portugal and local news of general interest to the Portuguese community in the USA.

The editor provided no tips for contributors.

Portuguese-American
LUSO-AMERICANO
Editors: A. Matinho and F. Cruz
88 Ferry Street
Newark
New Jersey 07105
(201) 589-4600
Publisher: Antonio Matinho
Established 1928
Sub.: U.S.:$20; International:$40
Distribution: Weekly
Cir.: U.S.:22,600; International:4,700
Portuguese, English text
99% non-English
Freelance articles accepted

SASE: No response
Ms.lang.: Not indicated
Query: No response
No ms.length indicted
Payment: No response
Photos/credits
Tabloid
Size: 10.25" x 15"
Black/white/color
Newsprint paper
White color paper
Display, classified
Deadline: Mondays
Outside group readers
"Kill" fee: No response

Luso-Americano is published in 99% Portuguese. No other information was provided.

Contributors would benefit from contacting the editors prior to submitting manuscripts.

R

Romanian
AMERICAN ROMANIAN REVIEW
Editor: Theodore Andrica
17313 Puritas Ave.
Cleveland
Ohio 44135
(216) 265-3532
Pub.: American Romanian Review
Established 1976
Subscription: U.S.:$10
Distribution: 6 times/year
Circulation: U.S.:600; International:80
English, Romanian text
5% non-English
Freelance articles accepted

SASE: No response
English ms.preference
Query: No response
No.ms.lgth.indicated
No payment
Photos/credits/no pay
Format: No response
Size: No response
Print process: No response
Paper type: No response
White color paper
No ads
Deadline: Not listed
Outside group readers
No "kill" fee

American Romanian Review is described as appealing mostly to American-born people of Romanian descent. The editor writes, "We are interested in material about the Romanians cultural and historical background including life in the USA and Canada."

Romanian
ROMANIAN BULLETIN
Romanian Library
200 E. 38th Street
New York, New York 10016
(212) 687-0180

The Romanian Bulletin ceased publication in 1981 according to the director of the Romanian Library.

Romanian, Romanian-American
NEW YORK SPECTATOR
Ed.Contact: Serban C. Andronescu
GCS Box 1364
New York City
New York 10163-1364
No telephone number
Pub.: Serban C. Andronescu
Established 1980
Subscription: U.S.:$25; International:optional
Distribution: Quarterly
Circulation: U.S.:1,800; International:200
Romanian, French, English text
50% non-English
Freelance articles accepted

SASE: Required
No ms.lang.prefer
Query, letter
No ms.length indicated
No pay/copies given
Photos/credits/no pay
Tabloid
Size: Not listed
Black/white
Newsprint paper
White color paper
Ads: No information
Deadline: Not listed
Outside gp.rdrs.: Unk.
No "kill" fee

New York Spectator publishes articles about cultural activities, Christian traditions, and Romanian-Americans for Romanian and French audiences.

The editor describes the editorial content as "conservative."

While the editor provided no tips for contributors, the following notation was made: "Ten to 25 copies of the newspaper are distributed to the addresses given by contributors (of articles)."

(Cross-referenced: Romanian-American.)

Romanian-American, Romanian
NEW YORK SPECTATOR
Ed.Contact: Serban C. Andronescu
GCS Box 1364
New York City
New York 10163-1364

See complete description and discussion in previous listing.

(Cross-referenced: Romanian.)

Russian-American
RUSSIAN LIFE
Editorial Board
2460 Sutter Street
San Francisco
California 94115
(415) 921-5380/(415) 921-5381
Pub.: Corporation "Russian Life" Inc.
Established 1921
Subscription: U.S.:$75/year
Distribution: Daily
Circulation: U.S.: 2,000
Russian text
100% non-English
Freelance articles accepted

SASE: Not indicated
Russian ms.prefer
Query, letter
No ms.length indicated
No payment
Photos/credits/no pay
Tabloid
Size: 8-12 pages
Black/white
Newsprint paper
Newsprint color paper
Display, classified
Deadline: Not listed
Libs., universities
No "kill" fee

Russian Life, published in the Russian language, is a daily tabloid which contains news, political analyses, essays, religion and science information. The audience is described as Russian-Americans.

The editorial representative did not provide any tips for contributors.

S

Scandinavian
SCANDINAVIAN REVIEW
Editor: Patricia McFate
127 East 73rd St.
New York
New York 10021
(212) 879-9779
Pub.: American-Scandinavian Found.,The
Established 1913
Sub.: U.S.:$15/yr.; International:$20/year
Distribution: Quarterly
Circulation: U.S.and International Total:5,000
English text
0% non-English
Freelance articles accepted

SASE: Required
English ms.preferred
Query, letter
No ms.length indicated
Payment/flat fee
No photos
Magazine
Size: 9.25" x 6"
Black/white/color
Glossy paper
White color paper
Display
Deadline: Request
Libraries receive
No "kill" fee

Scandinavian Review publishes articles about all five Scandinavian countries. The content of the articles is described as containing information on economics, politics, culture and the business of contemporary Nordic world.

The editor's advice to contributors: "Request editorial guidelines."

Deadline information for advertisers is available upon request.

Scandinavian
SVITHIOD JOURNAL
Editor: Betty Jane Clausen
5518 W. Lawrence Ave.
Chicago
Illinois 60640-3493
(312) 736-1191
Pub.: Indep.Order of Svithiod
Established September 1898
Subscription: U.S.: $1/year
Distribution: Monthly
Circulation: Controlled
English text
0% non-English
Freelance articles accepted

SASE: No response
English ms.preferred
Query: No response
No ms.length indicated
No pay
Photos/credits/no pay
Tabloid
Size: 8.5" x 11"
Black/white; Color Christmas
Newsprint paper
White color paper
No advertising
Deadline: Not specified
Exchange with other pub.
No "kill" fee

Svithiod Journal, as described by the editor, provides information to help readers keep abreast of happenings related to Scandinavian activities and information about culture and heritage of mainly Swedish traditions. The editor says there are occasional contributions from various officers and members of the Board of Directors of the Independent Order of Svithiod on topics of interest to members.

For freelance contributors the editor writes, "Hold articles to a reasonable length and no controversial topics."

Scandinavian
WITS & WITS II
Editor: Harald Naess
Dept. of Scandinavian Studies
University of Wisconsin
Madison, Wisconsin 53706
(608) 202-2090
Pub.: Dept.Scandinavian Studies
Established 1981
Subscription: No information
Distribution: Irregular
Circulation: No information
English text
0% non-English
No freelance accepted

SASE: No response
English ms.preference
Query: No response
Ms.length: 15,000 words
Payment: 50 copies
No photos
Pamphlet
WITS: 8.5" x 11; *WITS II*: 5.5" x 8"
Black/white
Paper type: Not listed
White color paper
No advertising
Deadline: Not listed
Interested persons receive
No "kill" fee

This publication is a pamphlet series, *WITS* 1,2,3 and WITS *II;* 1,2,3, for a total of six pamphlets in all as of 1987. The pamphlets are devoted to essays on Scandinavian language, history, geography, etc. *WITS,* and the second series, *WITS II,* focuses on translations of Scandinavian fiction.

The articles are usually solicited from specialists, and authors receive 50 copies of the pamphlet.

The length of articles published is usually 15,000 words. Occasionally, unsolicited material has been accepted for publication.

Scottish
SCOTIA NEWS
No longer published.

The publication address was listed as:

Macree
7154 Kessel Street
Forest Hills, N.Y. 11375

Scottish, Celtic, Irish, Welsh
THE DRAGON, THE THISTLE, THE HARP
Editor: J.D. Holsinger
2214 E. Cherryvale
Springfield
Missouri 65804
No phone listing
Pub.: Celtic Society of Missouri Ozarks
Established 1987
Subscription: Not listed
Distribution: Quarterly
Circulation: U.S.: 50
English text
% non-English: Minimal
Freelance accepted: Editor's decision

SASE: No response
Ms.lang.: No response
Query, letter
No ms.length indicated
Pay policy: No response
Photos: No response
Newsletter
Size: 8.5" x 11"-8.5" x 16"
Black/white
Regular bond paper
White color paper
Ads: None accepted
Deadline: Not listed
No outside group readers
"Kill" fee: No response

The Dragon, The Thistle, The Harp is a publication which, according to the editor, "tries to have articles on the Welsh, Scottish and Irish, especially in Missouri."

A sample of the publication contained articles about significant events, origin of Celtic names in the Ozarks, pronunciation technique discussion and news about members.

The editor writes that the publication has no experience with people "sending articles."

(Cross-referenced: Irish, Celtic, Welsh.)

Scottish-American
HIGHLANDER MAGAZINE, THE
Editor: Angus J. Ray
202 S.Cook Street; Suite 214
Barrington
Illinois 60010
(312) 382-1035
Publisher: Angus J.Ray Associates,Inc.
Established 1962
Subscription: U.S.:$10.50; Intl.:$12.50
Distribution: Bimonthly
Cir.: U.S.:37,000; International:2,000
English text
0% non-English
Freelance articles accepted

SASE: Required
English ms.preference
Query, letter
No ms.length indicated
Pay for freelance
Photos accepted/Pay
Magazine
Size: 8.375" x 10.25"
Black/white
Regular paper
White color paper
Display, classified
Deadline:15th-2nd.mo.bef.pub.
No outside group readers
No "kill" fee

The Highlander Magazine is written for Americans of Scottish descent and covers two fields of Scottish interest: (1) Activities of Scottish Societies in North America, and (2) Scottish history with emphasis on Scottish Clans and the role Scots have played in world history, particularly in North America.

With respect to "tips for contributors," the editor writes, "Fiction and poetry are not accepted. Articles should be related to Scotland in a time span of roughly 1300 to 1900."

Scottish-American
SCOTTISH-AMERICAN, THE
Editor: Donovan H. Bond
P.O.Box 397
Bruceton Mills
West Virginia 26525
(304) 379-8803
Publisher: W.R.McLeod
Established March 1983
Sub.: U.S.:$8; International:$12;varies
Distribution: Bimonthly
Cir.: U.S.:19,000; Intl.:1,000(Contl.)
English text
0% non-English
Freelance articles accepted

SASE: Not necessary
English ms.preference
Query unnecessary
No ms.length indicated
Payment, flat fee
Photos/credits/pay varies
Tabloid
Size: 10" x 12.5"
Black/white
Newsprint
White color paper
Display, classified
Deadline: 15th of alt.months
No outside group readers
"Kill" fee: Unknown

The Scottish-American is written for the Scottish-American community with corresponding interest in Britain, Australia, and so forth, according to the editor of the periodical.

In other information, the editor writes, "We cover Clan and Family Society activities, pertinent events in Scotland and Canada in which U.S. readers may have (an) interest, Scottish Highland Games in the U.S., with a small number in Canada as well, Scottish history and tradition, athletics, literature, music, dance. etc. We especially cover organizations which in turn promote the foregoing topics: St. Andrews Societies, Burns Societies, Scottish and Caledonian Societies, and so forth."

The editor says, "Brevity is essential in a tabloid; freshness and timeliness are essential in any newspaper."

Serbian
AMERICAN SRBOBRAN
Editor: Robert Rade Stone
3414 Fifth Avenue
Pittsburgh
Pennsylvania 15213
(412) 621-6600
Pub.: Serb National Federation
Established 1929
Sub.: U.S.:$40/yr; International:$42/year
Distribution: Weekly
Circulation: U.S.:6,000; Intl:1,000
Serbian, English text
50% non-English
Freelance articles accepted

SASE: No response
Serbianlang.ms.preferred
Query, letter
No ms.length indicated
No pay
No photos accepted
Newspaper
Size: Not listed
Black/white
Newsprint paper
White color paper
Display
Deadline: Monday noon
No outside group readers
"Kill" fee: No response

American Srbobran is described as a newspaper for readers of Serbian descent. The newspaper contains news about church, lodge activities, including choirs, ladies' groups and other Serbian organizations.

The editor provided no specific information for contributors.

Serbian
SERB WORLD U.S.A.
Editor: Mary Nicklanovich Hart
415 E. Mabel
Tucson
Arizona 85705
(602) 624-4887
Publisher: Serb World U.S.A. Inc.
Established 1979
Subscription: U.S.:$18; Intl.:$18
Distribution: Bimonthly
Circulation: U.S.:1960; Intl.:40
English text
0% non-English
Freelance articles accepted

SASE: No response
English ms.preference
Query unnec.;letter.o.k.
No ms.length indicated
No payment
Photos/cr./pay negotiated
Magazine
Size: 8.5" x 11"
Black/white
Paper: Bond
White color paper
Display, classified
Deadline: 1 month bef.pub.
University, public libraries
No "kill" fee

Serb World U.S.A. is, according to the editor, "A publication for and about Serbs living in America and Canada, especially 1st, 2nd and 3rd generation Americans with Serbian roots. We do historical pieces about our lives here in America and Canada and contemporary pieces. We also do historical pieces about our history in Yugoslavia."

Readers from outside the ethnic group include many university and public libraries, and individuals who are interested in Serbian ethnic history and immigration.

The editor describes the editorial content as "...not political and strictly secular."

The editor says the publication cannot pay writers, but that photographers come to an agreement regarding any payment.

The editor's tips to contributors: "Be interesting! Keep a general audience in mind. Write as though you were talking to them and decide what you want to tell them and what you want them to learn from your piece. Be patient with the publisher...there are many parts to a small publication, all to be tended by a small staff. Plan on several months before you get published."

Sicilian
ARBA SICULA/SICILIA PARRA
Editor: G. Giacchi
138 Bay 20th Street
Brooklyn
New York 11214-4620
(718) 331-0613
Publisher: Arba Sicula, Inc.
Established 1979/1980
Subscription: U.S.:$20; International:$20
Cir.: U.S.:1,250; International:250
Distribution: Quarterly
Sicilian, English text
50% non-English
Freelance articles accepted

SASE: No response
English, Sicilian ms.prefer
Query, letter
No ms.length indicated
No payment
Photos/credits
Magazine
Size: 6" x 9"; 8" x 11"
Color print: Not listed
Paper type: Not listed
Color paper: Not listed
Display, classified
Deadline: Irregular
Outside group readers
No "kill" fee

This periodical has two titles, *Arba Sicula/Scilia Parra* and is bilingual, that is, Sicilian language with English translation.

The editorial content is described as cultural, and the editor's tips to contributors: "Be scholarly."

Slavic
SLAVIC REVIEW
Editor: Ian Doric
16 S. Patterson Park Ave.
Baltimore
Maryland 21231
(301) 276-7676
Publisher: Slavic Convention
Established 1976
Subscription: U.S.:$5; International:$6
Distribution: Monthly
Circulation: U.S.:198,000; International:200
English text
0% non-English
Freelance articles accepted
SASE: No response
No manuscript lang.prefer
Query, letter
No ms.length indicated
Payment
Photos accepted/credits
Tabloid
Size: Not listed
Print color: Not listed
Newsprint paper
White color paper
Display, classified
Deadline: 15th of month
Some outside group readers
Pays "kill" fee

The editor describes the ethnic interests of *Slavic Review* as Slavic. No other information was provided.

Slavic-Polish
POLISH AMERICAN WORLD
Editor: L. Romalewski
3100 Grand Boulevard
Brooklyn
New York 11510
(516) 223-6514
Pub.: Thomas Poskropski
Established 1959
Subscription: U.S.:$12
Distribution: Weekly
Circulation: U.S.:10,000
English text
0% non-English
Freelance articles accepted
SASE: Required
English ms.preference
Query unnecessary
No ms.length indicated
No payment
Photos/credits/no pay
Newspaper
Size: Tabloid
Black/white
Newsprint paper
White color paper
Display, classified
Deadline: Monday
Outside group readers
No "kill" fee

Polish American World is published for the Slavic-Polish reader. No other information was provided.

Slovak
NARODNY NOVINY
Editor: Joseph Stefka
2325 E. Carson St.
Pittsburgh
Pennsylvania 15203
(412) 488-1890
Pub.: Natl. Slovak Society of USA
Established 1910
Subscription: $0 (Included in Membership)
Distribution: Monthly
Circulation: U.S.:11,500; International:400
Slovak, English text
25% non-English
Freelance not accepted/Staff assigned

SASE: Not applicable
Ms.lang.: No response
Query: Necessary; letter
No ms.length indicated
No pay
Photos: No response
Format: No response
Size: No response
Print process: No response
Paper type: No response
Paper color: Not listed
No ads accepted
Deadline: Not indicated
No outside group readers
No "kill" fee

Narodny Noviny is published for the Slovak Benefit Fraternal Society. It contains news about the membership and news of prominent Slovaks in the USA.

The editor says the editorials are slanted toward the membership, such as recruiting new members, urging volunteer service to charities, and so forth.

For prospective contributors, the editor writes, "We do not pay for freelance articles. We depend upon our own membership and the editorial staff to gather news of interest to our Slovak-American members."

Slovak
SLOVAK V AMERIKE
Editor: Draga Pauco
P.O. Box 150
Middletown
Pennsylvania 17057
(717) 944-0461
Publisher: Michael J. Krajsa
Established December 21, 1889
Subscription: U.S.:$15; International:$20
Distribution: Monthly
Circulation: U.S./International Total:1,200
Slovak text
98% non-English
Freelance: No response

SASE: No response
Slovak ms.preference
Query, letter
No ms.length indicated
Pay: No response
Print process: No response
Newspaper
Size: Not listed
Color paper: No response
Newsprint paper
White color paper
Display, classified
Deadline: 15th of month
Outside readers: Unknown
"Kill" fee: No response

Slovak V Amerike, as described by the editor: "Interests for Slovaks!" No other information provided for contributors.

Slovak Catholic
SLOVAK CATHOLIC FALCON
Editor: Daniel F. Tanzone
205 Madison Street
Passaic
New Jersey 07055
(201) 777-4010
Publisher: Slovak Catholic Sokol
Established April 15, 1911
Subscription: Members: Free; US/Intl.:$15
Distribution: Weekly
Circulation: U.S.:10,200; International:400
Slovak, English text
30% non-English
Freelance articles accepted

SASE: Not indicated
Ms.lang.not indicated
Query: Not indicated
No ms.length indicated
Pay/flat fee
No photos accepted
Tabloid
Size: 11.5" x 14.5"
Black/white
Newsprint paper
Buff color paper
Ads: No response
Deadline: Not listed
Univ./col.,other ethnic pub.
No "kill" fee

Slovak Catholic Falcon, titled "*Katolicky Sokol*" until January 1988, publishes information to promote the activity of the Slovak Catholic community in the United States and Canada. Additionally, this publication promotes the interests of the Slovak Catholic Sokol, its membership and the American and Canadian Slovak communities in general.

The editor had no suggestions for contributors.

Slovenian
ZARJA -- THE DAWN
Editor: Corinne Leskovar
431 N. Chicago
Joliet
Illinois 60432
(815) 727-1926
Pub.: Slovenian Women's Union of Amer.
Established 1928
Sub.: U.S.:$10;Intl.:No response
Distribution: 9 times/year
Circulation: U.S.:7,000
Slovenian, English text
25% non-English
No freelance accepted/Staff assigned

SASE: Not applicable
English ms.preference
Query, letter
Ms.guides to contributor
No payment
No photos/staff/credits
Magazine
Size: 8.5" x 11"
Black/white
Offset paper
White color paper
Display
Deadline:1st.of mo.b.pub.
No outside group readers
No "kill" fee

Zarja -- The Dawn is an "in-house" publication for the membership of the heritage-oriented women's organization, Slovenian Women's Union of America, which has deep ties to ethnic ancestry. The periodical is published in Slovenian and English. Contributors are members of the organization.

Regular contributors are advised of form, length of articles and so forth. The editors provided no other contributor's tips.

South American, Latin American, Cuban
LA TRIBUNA DE NORTH JERSEY
Editor: Humberto Perez
70 Kossuth Street
Newark
New Jersey 07101
(201) 589-3742
Publisher: Carlos Bidot
Established March 11, 1962
Subscription: U.S.:$25; (Controlled)
Distribution: Bimonthly
Circulation: U.S.:50,000 (total)
Spanish text
100% non-English
Freelance articles accepted/Agent referred

SASE: Required
Spanish ms.preference
Query, letter
No ms.length indicated
No payment
Photos/credits/no pay
Tabloid
Size: Not listed
B/W; Color spec.editions
Paper type: Not listed
White color paper
Display, classified
Deadline: Not listed
Colleges, businesses
No "kill" fee

La Tribuna de North Jersey publishes information for the Cuban exile community, Latin Americans and South Americans in the United States. The primary focus of the editorial content is human rights against dictatorship and against Communism.

The editor provided no tips for contributors.

(Cross-referenced: Cuban and Latin American.)

Spanish
NOTICIAS PARA LOS CALIFORNIANOS
Editor
P.O. Box 5155
San Francisco, California 94101

This periodical is not in publication at this time, 1988.

It is described as an "in-house" publication for Los Californianos, a non-profit organization. No other information was provided.

Spanish
PUNTO DE VISTA
Kent State University
Department of Romance Languages & Literature
Kent, Ohio 44242-0001
(216) 672-2150

Ceased publication in 1983.

Spanish
TEMAS
Editor: Jose De La Vega
1650 Broadway
New York
New York 10019
(212) 582-4750
Publisher: Jose De La Vega
Established 1950
Subscription: U.S.:$15; International:$22
Distribution: Monthly
Circulation: U.S.:110,000; Intl.:2,000
Spanish text
100% non-English
Freelance articles accepted

SASE: No response
Spanish manuscript preferred
Query, letter/phone
No manuscript length listed
Payment
Photos/credits/pay
Magazine
Size: 8.5" x 11"
Black/white/color
Glossy paper
White color paper
Display
Deadline: Not listed
Outside readers
No "kill" fee

Temas is described by the editor as a family magazine published in the Spanish language which features several topics, such as interviews with celebrities and artists, fashions, home decoration and current events of special interest for Spanish-speaking peoples.

No other information was provided.

Spanish
USA 23 MILLIONES
Editor: Thomas Fundora
3120 W. 8th Ave.
Hialeah
Florida 33012
(305) 588-0284
Publisher: Thomas Fundora
Established July 1981
Sub.: U.S.:$19.95; International:$40-60
Distribution: Monthly
Cir.: U.S.:61,000; Intl.:15,000
Spanish text
100% non-English
Freelance articles accepted

SASE: No response
Spanish ms.preference
Query: No response
No ms.length indicated
No payment
Photos/credits
Magazine
Size: Not listed
Black/white/color
Glossy paper
White color paper
Display
Deadline: 15th of month
No outside group readers
No "kill" fee

U.S.A. 23 Milliones is published in Spanish and dedicated to the world of Latin music.

The editor did not give any tips for contributors, but as with any publication, prospective contributors would most likely benefit from a review of the periodical prior to submitting manuscripts for consideration.

Spanish, Latin American
HISPANIC JOURNAL
Editor: Joseph B. Spieker
456 Sutton Hall
Indiana University of Pennsylvania
Indiana, Pennsylvania 15705
(412) 357-2327
Pub.: Dept.Span/Class.Languages
Established Fall 1979
Sub.: U.S.&Intl.:$8 indiv./inst.$12
Distribution: Biannual
Circulation: U.S.:400; International:200
Spanish, Portuguese, Catalan, English
50% non-English
Freelance articles accepted

SASE: Not required
Spanish, Engl.ms.preferred
Query unnecessary
No ms.length indicated
No payment
No photos/pay/credits
Magazine
Size: 8.75" x 5.75"
Black/white
Glossy paper
White color paper
No ads
Deadline: Not listed
Professors, univ.libraries
No "kill" fee

Hispanic Journal publishes, according to the editor, "articles examining primarily literary works of the Spanish and Latin American cultures which includes language, linguistics, history, art and culture of Hispano-America."

Although approximately half of the journal is published in Spanish, English is the other primary language used in the publication with some Portuguese and Catalan.

The length of the journal is from 150-200 pages.

The editor advises contributors to follow the *MLA Style Sheet* guidelines when submitting manuscripts for consideration.

(Cross-referenced: Latin American.)

T

Tibetan
NEWS TIBET
Editor
Old address:
Office of Tibet
301 E. 31st. Street
New York, New York 10016

The questionnaire was unclaimed at this address.

(Author's note: New information indicates the following: TIBET SOCIETY BULLETIN; Tibet Society, Inc.; Box 1968; Bloomington, Indiana. Phone: (812) 335-8222.)

U

Ukrainian
FORUM
Editor: Andrew Gregorovich
440 Wyoming Ave.
Scranton
Pennsylvania 18503
(717) 342-0937
Pub.: Ukrainian Fraternal Association
Established 1967
Sub.: U.S.$8; Intl.$9.50 (U.S.funds)
Distribution: Quarterly
Cir.: U.S./International:5,000+ total
English text
0% non-English
Freelance articles accepted

SASE: Not indicated
English ms.preference
Query: No response
No ms.length indicated
No payment
Photos/credits
Magazine
Size: 8.5" x 11"
Black/White, partial color
Glossy paper
White color paper
No advertising
Deadline: Not listed
Schools,libraries,museums
No "kill" fee

Forum publishes articles of history, cultural background, customs of Ukraine, information on the lives of historical leaders, artists and others.

The editor provided no other information.

Ukrainian
HARVARD UKRAINIAN STUDIES
Managing editor: Kathryn Taylor
1583 Massachusetts Ave.
Cambridge
Massachusetts 02138
(617) 495-4243
Pub.: Harvard Ukrainian Research Inst.
Established 1977
Sub.: U.S./Canada:$32;International $28
Distribution: Semi-annual
Circulation: U.S.:230; International:170
English text
5% non-English
Freelance:Not indicated

SASE: Not indicated
English ms.preferred
Query: No response
No ms.length indicated
Payment: No response
No photos
Format: No response
Size: 6" x 9"
Black/white
Paper type: Unknown
Buff color paper
Display: See below
Deadline: Unlisted
University libraries
No "kill" fee

Harvard Ukrainian Studies describes the ethnic interests of the publication as primarily Ukrainian, but Polish, Ukrainian relations with Eastern Europe and the inclusion of Ukrainian-Jewish questions also appear.

Although English is the primary language used in this periodical, the editor says that quotes and extracts appear in all Eastern European languages.

For contributors, the editors write, "Harvard Ukrainian Studies serves as a forum for new scholarship in Ukrainian studies. It deals primarily with history, language and literature. The journal cultivates an interdisciplinary approach that places Ukrainian topics in a broad scholarly context. It publishes articles, documents with analysis or interpretation, reviews articles and (other) reviews."

Ukrainian
HUTSYLIYA
Editor: N. Domashevsky
2453 W. Chicago Ave.
Chicago
Illinois 60622
(312) 267-7783
Publisher: Hutsul Association, Inc.
Established 1967
Sub.: U.S.:$10; Intl.:$10
Distribution: Quarterly
Circulation: U.S.:1,150; International:350
English, Ukrainian text
% non-English: No response
No freelance articles accepted

SASE: No response
No ms.lang.preference
Query: No response
No ms.length indicated
No pay for freelance
Photos: No credits/pay
Magazine
Size: Not listed
Black/white/color
Paper type: No response
Paper color: Unlisted
Classified
Deadline: Not listed
No outside group readers
No "kill" fee

Hutsyliya is described as, "dedicated to the study of Ukrainian ethnic Hutsul group, their land, history, art and culture. This includes activities of the Hutsul Association in the USA and Hutsul life in the Ukraine."

No suggestions for contributors were provided.

Ukrainian
NOVI NAPRIAMY/NEW DIRECTIONS
Editor
Old address:
140-142 Second Ave.
New York, New York 10003

The questionnaire was unclaimed, and no forwarding address was available.

Ukrainian
UKRAINIAN NATIONAL WORD
Editor: Larissa R. Masur
925 N. Western Ave.
Chicago
Illinois 60622
(312) 342-5103
Pub.: Ukrainian Natl.Aid Association
Established 1914
Subscription: Free to members
Distribution: Quarterly
Circulation: U.S.:2,932
Ukrainian, English text
95% non-English
No freelance accepted

SASE: No response
Ukrainian ms.preferred
Query, letter
No ms.length indicated
No pay
No photos
Tabloid
Size: Not listed
Black/white
Glossy paper
White color paper
Ads: No response
Deadline: Not listed
No outside group readers
No "kill" fee

Ukrainian National Word publishes information concerning the fraternal benefit society and Ukrainian politics. The articles are written by the staff of the periodical.

Ukrainian
UKRAINIAN WEEKLY, THE
Editor: Roma Hadzewycz
30 Montgomery St.
Jersey City
New Jersey 07302
(201) 434-0237
Publisher: Ukrainian National Association
Established 1933
Subscription: U.S.:$8; International:$8
Distribution: Weekly
Circulation: U.S.:6,000; Intl.:1,000
English text
0% non-English
Freelance articles accepted

SASE: Required
No ms.lang.preference
Query, letter
No ms.length indicated
Pay flat fee
Photos/credits
Tabloid
Size: Not listed
Black/white
Newsprint paper
Paper color: Unlisted
Ads: No response
Deadline: 1 week bef.pub.
Some outside gp.readers
No "kill" fee

The Ukrainian Weekly publishes everything from politics, history, to arts and people items. The news is about and of concern to Ukrainian and East European community members.

For contributing writers, the editor writes, "Become familiar with the content of the newspaper."

UKRAINICA EXILIANA
Editor: J.B. Rudnyckyj
Old address:
Institute of Exile Studies
1211 - 68th Ave.
Philadelphia, Pennsylvania 19126

The questionnaire was unclaimed, and no forwarding address was available.

Ukrainian (Boyko Land)
LITOPYS BOYKIWSHCHYNA
Editor: Myron Utrysko
2222 Brandywine St.
Philadephia
Pennsylvania 19130
(215) LO-7-3186 (as listed by ed.)
Publisher: Myron Utrysko
Established 1969
Subscription: U.S./International:$8 U.S.
Distribution: Bimonthly
Circulation: U.S.:410; International:190
Ukrainian text
100% non-English
No freelance accepted

SASE: No response
Ukrainian ms.preference
Query, no preference
No ms.length indicated
No payment
No photos accepted
Magazine
Size: Not listed
Black/white
Glossy paper
White, color cover
No ads
Deadline: Not listed
No outside group readers
No "kill" fee

Litopys Boykiwshchyna publishes research of history, culture and lives of Boyko Land and people. The people are of Ukrainian nationality.

According to the editor, a semi-annual issue is published which contains information about culture, history, arts, customary dress, language, biographies of famous Boyko people and information about Boykiwshchyna, region of the Ukraine.

Unknown
HAOR
Queens College
Student Union; Rm. B-43; Box 5
Flushing, New York 11367

This periodical is no longer in publication.

Unknown
L'N H/WHERE TO TONIGHT
Old address:
240 W. 73rd St.
New York, New York 10023

The questionnaire was unclaimed and no forwarding address was available.

Unknown
MENDY AND THE GOLEM
Old address:
450 Seventh Ave.
New York, New York 10001

The questionnaire package was "refused."

W

Welsh
CHICAGO DRAGON, THE
Editor: Myra Williams McWethy
c/o 1060 Fox Valley Drive
Aurora
Illinois 60504
No telephone listing
Pub.: Cambrian Benevolent Soc.of Chicago
Established January 1988
Subscription: U.S.:$1/year
Distribution: Quarterly
Circulation: No response
English, some Welsh text
.5% non-English
Freelance not accepted

SASE: No response
English ms.prefer
Query: No response
No ms.length indicated
No payment
No photos
Newsletter
Size: 8.5" x 11"
Black/white
Regular paper
White color paper
Display
Deadline: 3 weeks bef.pub.
Chicago Pub.Library
No "kill" fee

The Chicago Dragon contains Welsh news and information for the Chicagoland area. People profiles, local news, birth, death and anniversary notices are the kinds of news items sent in by readers. The editor says the publication is a "one person operation." The editor also writes the rest of the articles.

A sample copy was returned with the questionnaire, and it contained a variety of news items about events, past and up-coming, Welsh language opportunities and some genealogy notes.

Welsh
CYFEILLION MADOG
Editor: Evelyn Vandervelde
91 Le Mans Drive
Naples
Florida 33962
No telephone listing
Pub.: Welsh Studies Inst.of No.America
Established 1977
Sub.: Free to Welsh lang.supporters
Distribution: Biannual
Circulation: US:300; International:300
English, Welsh text
1% non-English
Freelance articles accepted

SASE: Not required
English ms.prefer
Query unnecessary
No ms.length indicated
No payment
Photos/no credits/no pay
Tabloid
Size: 8.5" x 11"
Black/white
Bond paper
White color paper
No advertising
Deadline: Not indicated
Linguists, researchers
No "kill" fee

Cyfeillion Madog is, according to the editor, dedicated to the furtherance of the Welsh language in North America, and specifically used to promote the yearly Welsh language course, Cwrs Cymraeg held in July or August on a college campus in the United States or Canada.

The publication is further described as non-political, but stresses the importance of the Welsh language to the survival of Welsh history and culture.

The editor asks that articles be "well-written, short and pursuant to the purpose of the paper."

(Author's note: Contributors would benefit from reading a copy of the paper. Don't forget the SASE.)

Welsh
IOWA WELSH SOCIETY
Editor: Nancy Evans
1009 Highland
Red Oak
Iowa 51566
No telephone listing
Publisher: Iowa Welsh Society
Established 1985
Sub.:U.S.:$3/yr.Membership
Distribution: Infrequent
Circulation: Controlled
English text
0% non-English
Freelance articles accepted

SASE: Recommended
English ms.preference
Query, letter
No ms.length indicated
No payment
Photos: Rarely used
Newsletter
Size: 8.5" x 11"
Black/white
Bond paper
White color paper
No advertising
Deadline: Not listed
No outside group readers
No "kill" fee

This publication, *Iowa Welsh Society*, is an information newsletter for members. Both the newsletter and the Iowa Welsh Society are new, established in 1985, and it is still in the formative stages of organization.

A sample newsletter contained information about a Welsh language course, St.David's Day celebration (March 1), as well as meeting information and news of members' contributions.

Articles sent to the editor should have a strong Welsh angle, preferably with an Iowa slant.

(Author's note: This information provided by the author.)

Welsh
NINNAU
Editor: Arturo L. Roberts
11 Post Terrace Road
Basking Ridge
New Jersey 07920
(201) 766-6736
Publisher: Arturo L. Roberts
Established November l, 1975
Sub.:U.S.:$14; Canada:$ 14; U.K. 9
Distr.: Monthly, except Sept.
Cir.: U.S.:4,500; International:500
English, Welsh Text
5% non-English
Freelance articles accepted
SASE: Not required
English ms.preference
Query telephone O.K.
No ms.length indicated
No payment
Photos/credits/no pay
Tabloid
Size: 11.5" x 15"; 28 pages
Black/white
Newsprint paper
White color paper
Display
Deadline: 15th of prior mo.
No outside group readers
No "kill" fee

Ninnau, pronounced, "nin-eye," means "us or we also," publishes articles to inform the North American Welsh about local and general news of interest, support community activities, publicizes individual contributions to community life, provides forum for discussion, educates in Welsh traditions and is seen as an information link within North America and with Wales.

According to the editor, the publication provides news of Welsh activities in the United States and Canada. Stories about well-known North American Welsh, Welsh language lessons, news from Wales, columns on Welsh cooking and genealogy, feature stories, travel page, calendar of coming events, advertisements by Welsh stores and services.

The editor suggests that contributors "call or drop us a line."

Welsh
Y DRYCH
Editor: Patricia Powell Viets
P.O. Box 369
De Pere
Wisconsin 54115
(414) 336-9630
Publisher: Patricia Powell Viets
Established January 1, 1851
Subscription: U.S.:$15; International:$20
Distribution: Monthly
Cir.: U.S./International Total: 4,000
English, Welsh text
% non-English: Minimal
Freelance articles accepted

SASE: Not required
English ms.preference
Query unnecessary
No ms.length listed
Pay: Editor's decision
Photo/credits/pay
Tabloid
Size: 11" x 16"
B/W; 1 color occasionally
Newsprint
White color paper
Display, classified
Deadline: 10th of month
Outside group readers
No "kill" fee

Y Drych is North America's oldest ethnic newspaper which has been in continuous publication since it began in 1851, according to editor and publisher, Patricia Powell Viets.

The ethnic interests of the publication reflect all aspects of Welsh life, current events in Wales, activities of Welsh organizations in North America, personal experiences with a Welsh background, personality profiles, genealogy, Welsh books (reviews and serialized), opinion essays, scenic photographs of Wales.

Payment of freelance articles and photographs is sometimes given at the discretion of the editor.

The editor gives these tips for contributors: "Lively, human interest stories which, of course, must have a Welsh slant; travel articles with a Wales locale."

Author's update: All inquiries should be directed to the new editor/publisher, Mary Morris Mergenthal; P.O. Box 8089; St. Paul, Minnesota 55108.

Welsh, Irish, Celtic, Scottish
THE DRAGON, THE THISTLE, THE HARP
Editor: J.D. Holsinger
2214 E. Cherryvale
Springfield
No phone listing
Pub.: Celtic Society of Missouri Ozarks
Established 1987
Subscription: Not listed
Distribution: Quarterly
Circulation: U.S.:50
English text
% non-English: Minimal
Freelance accepted: Editor's decision

SASE: No response
Ms.lang.: Not indicated
Query, letter
No ms.length indicated
Pay: No response
Newsletter
Size: 8.5" x 11" to 16"
Black/white
Bond regular paper
White color paper
No ads accepted
No deadline listed
No outside group readers
"Kill" fee: No response

The Dragon, The Thistle, The Harp is a publication which, according to the editor, "tries to have articles on the Welsh, Scottish and Irish, especially in Missouri."

A sample of the publication contained articles about significant events, origin of Celtic names in the Ozarks, pronunciation technique discussion and news about members.

The editor says the publication has no experience with people "sending articles."

(Cross-referenced: Celtic, Irish, Scottish.)

Y

Yiddish
AFN SHVEL (ON THE THRESHOLD)
Editor: Mordkhe Schaechter
200 West 72 St.; No. 40
New York
New York 10023
(212) 787-6675
Publisher: League for Yiddish
Established 1941
Subscription: U.S.: $6; International:$8
Circulation: U.S.:1,000;International:300
Distribution: Quarterly
Yiddish text
100% non-English
Freelance articles accepted

SASE: No response
Yiddish ms.preferred
Query: No response
No ms.length indicated
No pay freelance
Photos/credits/no pay
Magazine
Size: 8" x 11"
Black/white
Paper type: Regular
White color paper
Display
Deadline: 4 wks.bef.pub.
Interested in Yiddish
No "kill" fee

Afn Shvel is written and published for the Yiddish-speech community according to the editor of the magazine, and non-ethnic interest readers are described as those non-Jews interested in Yiddish. The editorial content is described as "cultural Yiddishist."

The editor did not provide any suggestions for prospective contributors, but as with most periodicals, freelance contributors would probably benefit from reviewing a copy of the publication prior to submitting materials for consideration.

Yiddish
KULTUR UN LEBN
Editor: Joseph Mlotek
45 E. 33rd. Street
New York
New York 10016
(212) 889-6800
Publisher: Workmen's Circle
Established 1967
Subscription: Controlled
Distribution: Quarterly
Circulation: U.S.: 25,000
Yiddish text
100% non-English
No freelance accepted

SASE: Not applicable
Yiddish ms.preference
Query: Not applicable
Ms.lgth.: Not applicable
Payment: Not applicable
No freelance photos
Magazine
Size: 8" x 10.75"
Black/white,some color
Regular paper
White color paper
No advertising
Deadline: Not indicated
Some outside readers
"Kill" fee: Not applicable

Kultur un Lebn is a journal meant to serve members of the Workmen's Circle who are Yiddish readers and speakers.

The content deals with issues within the organizational sphere of interest, and for Yiddish readers, the text is Yiddish.

Yiddish
YUGNTRUF-Youth for Yiddish
Editor: Paul Glasser
3328 Bainbridge Ave.
Bronx
New York 10467
(212) 654-8540
Publisher: YUGNTRUF-Youth for Yiddish
Established 1964
Sub.: U.S.: Students:$5; Others:$10
Distribution: Quarterly
Circulation: U.S.:2,200
Yiddish text
100% non-English
Freelance articles accepted

SASE: No response
Yiddish ms.preference
Query: No response
No ms.length indicated
No payment
Photos/credits
Magazine
Size: 9.5" x 6"
Black/white
Regular bond paper
White color paper
Display
Deadline: Not listed
Libraries
"Kill" fee: No response

YUGNTRUF-Youth for Yiddish is published for a readership which is interested in Yiddish language and culture. The editor describes it as non-partisan, Yiddish, and asks that contributors submit articles written in Yiddish.

Yugoslavian, Croatian
ZAJEDNICAR (The Fraternalist)
Editor: Edward J. Verlich
100 Delaney Dr.
Pittsburgh
Pennsylvania 15235
(412) 351-3909
Pub.: Croatian Fraternal Union of America
Established 1904
Subscription: Controlled-Members only
Distribution: Weekly
Cir.: U.S.:33,000; International:7,000
Croatian and English text
35-40% non-English
Freelance acceptance: Editor's decision

SASE: No response
English ms. prefer
Query: No response
No ms.length indicated
No payment
Photos/no pay
Tabloid
Size: 11.5" x 16.5"
Black/white/color
Newsprint paper
White color paper
No advertising
Deadline:Unknown
No outside readers
No "kill" fee paid

Zajednicar seeks to inform its membership of the events in the Croatian Fraternal Union of America. Additionally, the periodical publishes information to help preserve and promote Croatian heritage and culture; keep the membership informed of the events in Croatia and Yugoslavia, promote Croatian art, music and culture as well as encourage and publish events of the junior and adult tamburitza ensembles.

The editorial content is described as containing news, human interest articles and feature stories with ample pictorial display of members, lodges, national officers, National Administration, central committees, junior and adult tamburitzans, Croatia and Yugoslavia.

The editor comments, "We reserve the right to edit, change, add and delete. You can contribute completed story or just give us the facts, and we'll do the rest."

(Cross-referenced: Croatian.)

Z

Zionist
ALIYON
Editor: Anita Levor
515 Park Ave.
New York City
New York 10022
(212) 752-0600
Pub.: North American Aliya Movement
Established 1968
Sub.: U.S.:$20-25 (contl.members)
Distribution: Quarterly
Circulation: U.S.:4,700; International:300
English, Hebrew text
3% non-English
Freelance articles accepted

SASE: No response
English ms.preference
Query unnec.; letter O.K.
No ms.length indicated
No pay
Photos/credits
Magazine
Size: 8.25" x 10.75"
Black/white
Newsprint paper
White color paper
Display, classified
Deadline: Not listed
Zionist, Jewish leaders
No "kill" fee paid

Aliyon is a Zionist publication: Aliya (Immigration to Israel) oriented ideology, technical and cultural information. Technical refers to information about buying appliances for Israel, which region to settle in, shipping your personal effects, and so forth.

Prospective contributors should consider personal interest in *Aliyon* coupled with clear writing/art ability.

Zionist
YIDDER KEMFER
Editor: M. Strigler
275-7th Ave.; 17th floor
New York City
New York 10001
(212) 675-7808
Publisher: Labor Zionist Letters,Inc.
Established May 1906
Subscription: U.S.:$30; International:$30
Distribution: Weekly
Circulation: U.S.:2,250; International:550
Yiddish, English text
0% non-English
Freelance articles accepted

SASE: No response
English ms.prefer
Query: No response
No ms.length indicated
No payment
No photos accepted
Magazine
Size: Not listed
Black/white
Glossy paper
White color paper
Display
Deadline: Friday
No outside group readers
"Kill" fee: No response

The editorial content of *Yidder Kemfer* is described as labor, Zionism. The editor provided no tips for contributors.

Zionist, Jewish
HADASSAH MAGAZINE
Executive Editor: Alan M. Tigay
50 West 58th Street
New York
New York 10019
(212) 303-8014
Pub.: Hadassah;Women's Zion.Org.
Established 1914
Sub.: U.S.:$1.50/issue (Controlled)
Distribution: Ten issues/year
Cir.: U.S.:360,000; Intl.:0
English text
0% non-English
Freelance articles accepted
SASE: Required
English ms.preference
Query, letter
No ms.length indicated
Pay/fl.fee; most articles asgn.
Photos/pay/credits
Magazine
Size: 8.5" x 11"
Black/white/color
Glossy paper
White color paper
Display, classified
Deadline: 18th of sec.mo.b.pub.
Libraries
No "kill" fee

Hadassah is a Zionist Jewish organization, therefore, the magazine's interests focus primarily on Jewish life in America and Israel.

The editor of *Hadassah Magazine* writes: "We have regular columns on political questions that affect Jews in America and Israel, Jewish parenting, travel and the arts. There is a regular column on the Hadassah-Hebrew University Hospital in Jerusalem and a book review section for fiction and non-fiction that deals with Jewish topics. We use two to three feature length articles per month and accept short fiction as well."

Payment for freelance articles and photographs is given, although freelance photographs are rarely accepted since most are assigned. Cover photographs (color transparency) payment is $175; Black and White inside:$50 and $30 for each additional photo in one article. Check with the editor regarding selection and payment rate policies on freelance photographs.

(Cross-referenced: Jewish.)

Zionist, Jewish
HERZL INSTITUTE BULLETIN
Editor
515 Park Avenue
New York
New York 10022
No phone listing
Publisher: Theodor Herzl Institute
Established: No information
Sub.: Member:Individual:$20; Couple:$35
Distribution: Biweekly
Circulation: No information
English text
%non-English: No response
Freelance articles not accepted

SASE: No information
Ms.lang.: No response
Query: See description
No ms.length indicated
Payment: No information
Photos used
Size: 7" x 10"
Bulletin
Black/white
Bond paper
White color paper
No ads
Deadline: Not listed
No outside group readers
"Kill fee": No response

The *Herzl Institute Bulletin* and *Seasonal Preview* booklet are published by The Theodor Herzl Institute. The Institute's purpose and policy, published in the Seasonal Preview booklet states:

> "The Theodor Herzl Institute, sponsored by the World Zionist Organization-American Section, is a center for adult Zionist education. Through a wide range of educational activities, the Institute fosters a greater understanding of contemporary Jewish problems here and abroad, examines the values and precepts of the Jewish Heritage, encourages the study of modern Israel, and engages in social research in areas of Jewish interest.
>
> "The spirit of free inquiry guides all Institute activities. It is bound by no commitment to any particular Zionist ideological orientation. The scope of its work encompasses the broad range of Jewish interests, with particular consideration given to the history and impact of Zionism--the national liberation movement of the Jewish people, which culminated in the creation of the State of Israel."

According to the response to the questionnaire, queries should pertain to membership information or program offerings only. Respondent requested that no other queries be sent.

(Cross-referenced: Jewish.)

Appendix A

LIST OF NON-RESPONDING ETHNIC-INTEREST PERIODICALS

The following periodicals were included in the second mailing, but did not respond to the second request for information. This list is provided as a point of information only. Readers who are interested in these periodicals should query before sending any manuscripts.

AJC REVIEW
C. Berlin, Editor
900 Jefferson St.; No. 6249
Arcadia, CA 91006

ASA NEWS - UCLA
E.Huckaby, Ed., 255 Kinsey Hall
405 Hilgard Ave.
Los Angeles, CA 90024

ASA PAPERS-UCLA
Editor; 255 Kinsey Hall
405 Hilgard Ave.
Los Angeles, CA 90024

ASC NEWSLETTER
L. Kapteijns, Editor
Michigan State University
100 Center for Intl.Programs
East Lansing, MI 48824

ABOUT...TIME
C.S.Blount, Editor
30 Genesee St.
Rochester, NY 14611

AD KAAN
B. Mann, Editor
50 W. 58th Street
New York, NY 10019

AFRICAN CONNECTION NEWSPAPER
W.Boynes, Ed. & Pub.
12 W. 21st St.; 11th Floor
New York, NY 10010

AFRICAN ENQUIRER
African Enquirer Publications
C.A. Onyeani, Editor
463 N.Arlington Ave.
East Orange, NJ 07017

AM-POL EAGLE
M.W. Pelczynski, Ed/Pub.
1335 E. Delavan Ave.
Buffalo, NY 14215

AMERICAN CROAT
R.P.Radielovic, Ed./Pub.
Box 3025
Acadia, CA 91006

AM.ETHNIC HISTORY, JOURNAL OF
R.H.Bayor, Editor
Rutger's University
New Brunswick, NJ 08903

ADELANTE (ORLANDO)
A.F. Hernandez, Ed. & Pub.
Box 811
Orlando, FL 32802

AMERICAN JEWISH LIFE
S.D. Jacobs, Editor
Box 207
West Trenton, NJ 08062

ANALYSIS OF JEWISH POLICY
Editor-in-Chief
Synagogue Council of America
327 Lexington Ave.
New York, NY 10016

ARIZONA INDIAN MONTHLY
B.Coates, Ed./Pub.
1777 W.Camelback Road
A-108
Phoenix, AZ 85105

ARMENIAN DIGEST
H.Tankian, Editor
Gulf Publishing Ltd.
GPO Box 2754
New York, NY 10116

ARROW (ASHLAND)
Editor
St.Labre Indian School
Ashland, MT 59003

BAND MAGAZINE
Jeannette Hodge, Ed./Pub.
143-14 Lakewood Ave.
Jamaica, NY 11435

BLACK-JEWISH INFO.CENTER
Media Project
Ron Kaplan, Editor
16 East 85th Street
New York, NY 10028

BLACK NATION
A.Baraka, Editor
Box 29293
Oakland, CA 94604

B'NAI B'RITH MESSENGER
Rabbi Y.B.Butler, Editor
2510 W. 7th Street
Los Angeles, CA 90057

BORO PARK VOICE
A.Friedlander, Editor
4616 13th Avenue
Brooklyn, NY 11229

BRIDGE: ASIAN AMERICAN PERSPECTIVES
Editorial Board
32 East Broadway
New York, NY 10002

BRIDGES
D.Jonaitis, Editor
314 Highland Blvd.
Brooklyn, NY 11207

CAA NEWSLETTER
Editor
17 Walter U.Lum Place
San Francisco, CA
92108-1801

CALIFORNIA ADVOCATE NEWSPAPER
L.Kimber, Editor
Box 11826
Fresno, CA 93775

CAMPANA
E.Athanasiares, Editor
600 W. 188th Street
New York, NY 10040

CARTA ABIERTA
J.Rodriguez, Editor
Texas Lutheran College
Mexican American Studies
Sequin, Texas 78155

CHINESE HISTORICAL SOCIETY
Editorial Board
17 Adler Place
San Francisco, CA 94133

CINCINNATI HERALD
c/o Editor
863 Lincoln Ave.
Cincinnati, OH 45206

CIRCLE (JAMAICA PLAIN)
Editor
Boston Indian Council
105 S. Huntington Ave.
Jamaica Plain, MA 02130

COLUMBUS TIMES
O. Mitchell, Editor
4650 Down Court
Columbus, GA 31907

CONCH
Editor
P.O. Box 777
Buffalo, NY 14213-0777

DAVKA
N.Reisner, Editor
900 Hilgard Ave.
Los Angeles, CA 90024

DAWN MAGAZINE
R.W.Matthews, Editor
628 N.Eutaw St.
Baltimore, MD 21203

DE COLORES
J.Armas, Editor
2633 Grantite N.W.
Box 7264
Albuquerque, NM 87104

DENVER WEEKLY NEWS
F.C.Harris, Editor
2547 Welton St.
Denver, CO 80205

DER DEUTSCH-AMERIKANER
Editor
4740 N.Western Ave; 2nd.Fl.
Chicago, IL 60625

DIRVA
V.Gedgaudas, Editor
6116 St.Clair Ave.
Cleveland, OH 44103

EAST ST.LOUIS MONITOR
A.L.Sanders, Editor
1501 State Street
Box 2137
East St. Louis, IL 62292

EAST WIND
E.Wong, Editor
Box 29293
Oakland, CA 94604

ESSENCE
S.L.Taylor, Editor
1500 Broadway
New York, NY 10036

FFP BULLETIN
J.Kaufmann, Editor
Box 2125
Durham, NC 27702

FAMILIA LATINA
Magdalena Gonzalez, Editor
1219 Palo Verde
Carson City, NV 89701-4338

FOCUS MAGAZINE (Hartford)
W.R.Hales, Editor
3281 Main Street
Hartford, CT 06120

FORUMEER
L.W.Gonzalez, Editor
621 Gabaldon Rd., N.W.
Albuquerque, NM 87104

FORT APACHE SCOUT
J.A.Vicario, Editor
Box 1255
Pinetop, AZ 95935

FORWARD TIMES
c/o L.Carter
4411 Almeda Road
Houston, TX 77004

FREEDOMWAYS
E.Jackson/J.Carey, Eds.
799 Broadway; Ste. 542
New York, NY 10003

An GAEL
Irish Arts Center
K.T.McEneaney, Editor
553 W.51st. Street
New York, NY 10019

GENTLEMEN OF COLOR
Editor
Thomas Rivers Pub.Co.
P.O.Box 142
Matteson, IL 60443-0142

GLOBE (FLUSHING)
Editors
City Univ. of New York
65-30 Kissena Blvd.
Flushing, NY 11367

GREEK ACCENT
Greek Accent Pub.Corp.
S.Phillips, Exec.Ed.
41-47 Crescent St.
Long Island, NY 11101

HAMAGSHIMIM JOURNAL
B.Mann, Editor
50 W.58th St.
New York, NY 10019

HAUSFRAU, DIE
Editors
1060 Gaines School Rd.
Ste.B-3
Athens, GA 30605-3136

HELLENIC TIMES, THE
265 West 87th Street
2nd.Floor
New York, NY 10024-2750

HILLEL GATE
Editors; Brooklyn College
B'nai B'rith Hillel Found.
Brooklyn College
2901 Campus Road
Brooklyn, NY 11210

HISPANIC LINK WEEKLY REPORT
F.Perez, Editor
1420 N.St.N.W.
Washington, D.C. 200015

IDE JOURNAL
Chairperson, Editorial Bd.
850 Third Ave.; Ste.607
New York, NY 10022

I LAISVE/TOWARD FREEDOM
V.Rochiunas, Editor
1634 - 49th Avenue
Cicero, IL 60650

INDIA-AMERICAN SOCIETY BULLETIN
c/o Sushila Janadass, Editor
4318 Rhode Ave.
Studio City, CA 91604-1633

INDIAN TRUTH
S.Glazer, Editor
1505 Race Street
Philadelphia, PA 19102

INDIANA JEWISH POST AND OPINION
E.Stattmann, Editor
2129 N.Meridian
Indianapolis, IN 46202

INFORMADOR
C.Cavarro, Editor
1510 W. 18th St.
Chicago, IL 60608

IRISH PEOPLE (NEW YORK)
M.Galvin, Editor
4951 Broadway
New York, NY 10034

ISRAEL TODAY
P.Blazer, Editor
Box 1909 - 245
Van Nuys, CA 91405

ITALIAN AMERICANA
Editors
1300 Elmwood Ave.
Buffalo, NY 14222

JEWISH CHICAGO
Editor
7008 N.California
Chicago, IL 60645-3029

JEWISH CURRENT EVENTS
S.Deutsch, Editor
430 Keller Ave.
Elmont, NY 11003

JEWISH EXECUTIVE
M.Milstein, Editor
112 Broadway
Malverne, NY 11735-3919

JEWISH EXPONENT
A.Erlick, Editor
226 S. 16th St.
Philadelphia, PA 19102

JEWISH HERALD-VOICE
J.& J.Samuel, Editors
3403 Audley, Box 153
Houston, TX 77001

JEWISH LEADER
V.Shulman, Editor
1 Bulkeley Place
New London, CT. 06320-6206

JEWISH LEDGER
B.Morganstern, Editor
3385 Brighton
Henrietta Townline Rd.
Rochester, NH 14623-2842

JEWISH PEOPLE
W.E.Rapfogel, Editor
110 East 23rd.
New York, NY 10010

JEWISH POST AND OPINION
G.Cohen, Editor
2120 N.Meridian St.
Indianapolis, IN 46202

JEWISH PRESS (BROOKLYN)
S.Klass, Editor/Publisher
338 Third Ave.
Brooklyn, NY 11215

JEWISH RECORD
M.Korik, Editor
1537 Atlantic Ave.
Atlantic City, NY 08401

JEWISH STANDARD
M.J.Janoff, Editor
385 Prospect Ave.
3rd.Floor
Hackensack, NJ 07601

JEWISH WEEK
S.Engelmayer, Editor
1457 Broadway
New York, NY 10036

JEWISH WEEKLY NEWS
L.B.Kahn, Editor
Box 1569
Springfield, MA 01101

JOURNAL HALACHA AND CONTEMPORARY SOCIETY
Rabbi A.Cohen, Editor
3495 Richmond Road
Staten Island, NY 10306

KAHANE
Editor
Midwood Station; Box 425
Brooklyn, NY 11230

KANSAS CITY JEWISH CHRONICLE
Ruth Bigus, Editor
7373 W. 107th Street
Overland Park, KS 66217

KENTUCKY JEWISH POST AND OPINION
G.Cohen, Editor
1551 Bardstown Road
Louisville, KY 40205

KOL H-T'HUANH/VOICE OF THE MOVEMENT
J.Levine, Editor
50 W. 58th Street
New York, NY 10019

LAIKS
I.Spilners, Editor
7307 Third Avenue
Brooklyn, NY 11209

LAS VEGAS ISRAELITE
M.Tell, Editor
Box 14096
Las Vegas, NV 89114

LEVIATHAN
A.Caspi, D.Pulcrano, Eds.
Redwood Bldg.
University of California
Santa Cruz, CA 95604

LIFE AND SCHOOL
Dr.W.O.Luciw, Editor
418 W.Nittany Ave.
State College, PA 16801

LINCOLN REVIEW
J.A.Parker, Editor
1001 Connecticut Ave. N.W.
Suite 1135
Washington, D.C. 20036

LONG ISLAND JEWISH WORLD
N.Lippman, Editor
115 Middle Neck Road
Great Neck, NY 11201

MALDEF NEWSLETTER
Mexican-Amer.Legal Defense Education Fund
634 Spring Street; 11 Floor
Los Angeles, CA 90014

MABUEY HANCHAL
Rabbi M.Turetz, Editor
35 Lee Ave.
Brooklyn, NY 11211

MACON COURIER
L.D.Wilder, Editor
2661 Montpelier Ave.
Macon, GA 31204

MAGYAR HOLNAP/ HUNGARIAN TOMORROW
Box 441; Gracie Station
New York, NY 10028

MALINI
C.Chakraborty, Editor
Box 195
Claremont, CA 91711

MASHRIQ
H.Yatooma, Editor
15 E. 84th Street
New York, NY 10010

MEDIA INFORMATION BULLETIN
J.Schatz, Editor
15 E. 84th Street
New York, NY 10010

MEDIUM
E.A.Goldman, Editor
15 E. 84th Street
New York, NY 10010

MEIE TEE
H.Raudsepp, Editor
243 East 34th St.;Box 123
New York, NY 10016

MIDDLE EAST MEMO
R.Cohen, Editor
515 Park Avenue
New York, NY 10022

MIDSTREAM
J.Carmichael, Editor
515 Park Ave.
New York, NY 10022

MILWAUKEE HERALD
Editor
2321 W. Kenboern Dr.
Glendale, WI 53209

MISSOURI JEWISH POST AND OPINION
K.Sutin, Editor
9531 Lackland Road; No.207
St. Louis, MO 63114-3602

MWENGE
J.M. Muganda, Editor
2139 R.St. N.W.
Washington, D.C. 20008

NATIVE HAWAIIAN
Editor
1024 Mapunapuna
Honolulu, HI 96819-3297

NAACP NEWSLETTER
D.L.Watson, Editor
4805 Mt. Hope Dr.
Baltimore, MD 21215-3297

NATIONAL JEWISH ARTS NEWSLETTER
C.Miller, Editor
15 E. 84th Street
New York, NY 10028

NAVAJO AREA NEWSLETTER
F.D.Hardwick, Editor
Navajo Area Office;Box M
Window Rock, AZ 86515

NAVAJO TIMES TODAY
M.N.Trahant, Editor
Box 310
Window Rock, AZ 86515

NEGRO HISTORY BULLETIN
B.J.Gillespie, Editor
1407 - 14th St.N.W.
Washington, D.C. 20005

NEW AL-HODA
F.K.Stephen, Editor
34 W.28th Street
New York, NY 10001

NEW DIMENSIONS
(Philadelphia)
M.M.Stolarik, Editor
18 S. Seventh St.
Philadelphia, PA 19106

NEW HORIZON
Polish American Review
B.Wierzbianski, Editor
21 W. 38th St.
New York, NY 10018

NEW JERSEY AFRO-AMERICAN
R.Queen, Editor
Box 22162
Newark, NJ 07101-2162

NEW KOREA
Woon-Ha Kim, Editor
2936 W. 8th Street
Los Angeles, CA 90007

NEW TIMES (Rock Island)
M.M.Thomas, Editor
1000 - 21st St.
Rock Island, IL 61201

NIGHT MOVES
H.Wilson, Editor
105 W.Madison; Ste. 1100
Chicago, IL 60602

NINGAS
N.A.Navarro, Editor
17 E. 16th Street; 4th Floor
New York, NY 10003

NORTH AMERICAN INDIAN
J.Rochford, Editor
10186 Hooper Street
San Diego, CA 92124

NORTHERN CALIFORNIA
JEWISH BULLETIN
M.S.Klein, Editor
121 Stuart Street; No.302
San Francisco, CA 94105

NOTICIAS DE AZTLAN
T.Gaspar, Editor
UCLA-Chicano Studies
Research Center
Los Angeles, CA 9002

NOVY ZHURNAL/NEW
REVIEW
R.Goul, Editor
611 Broadway; No. 842
New York, NY 10025

NUESTRO ENCUENTRO
Editor
Anti-Defamation League
B'nai B'rith
823 United Nations Plaza
New York, NY 10017

OIO NEWS
I.Hayden, Editor
555 Constitution
Norman, OK 73069

OH HI YOH NOH
Editor
Seneca Nation of Indians
Box 231; Plumber Building
Salamanaca, NY 14779

OTHER BLACK WOMAN
Editor
72-15 41st Ave.
Station D 43
Jackson Heights, NY 11372

OUR LIFE
O.Liskiwsky, Editor
UNWLA, Inc.
108 Second Ave.
New York, NY 10003

OUTREACH (NEW YORK)
M.Ashjian, Editor
Armenian Apostolic Church
of America
138 E. 39th Street
New York, NY 10016

PAMIR MAGAZINE/PA MI ERH
ZAZHI
Chinese Cultural Association
P.Cieh Wang, Editor
8122 Mayfield Rd.;Box 8
Chesterland, OH 44026

PAMOJA TUTASHINDA
Editorial Bd. Chairperson
Williams College
Student Union 639
Williamstown, MA 01267

PERSPECTIVES
J.Yellin, Editor
Columbia University
105 Earl Hall
New York, NY 10027

PERSPECTIVES
(WASHINGTON)
K.Kusielewicz, Editor
700 7th Street. S.W.
Washington, D.C. 20041

PEYVAND
G.R.Sami, Editor
Bita Publishing Co.
Box 1929
Falls Church, VA 20041

QUA' TOQUI
Hopi Publishers
A.Sekaquaptewa, Editor
Box 266
Oraibi, AZ 86039

RAIVAAJA/PIONEER
M.Cautnen, Editor
Raivaaja Publishing Co.
147 Elm; Box 600
Fitchburg, MA 01420

RAWHIDE PRESS
M.L.Wynn, Editor
Box 373
Willpinit, WA 00940

RECENZIJA Editor
Harvard Ukrainian Research
Institute
1581-83 Massachusetts Ave.
Cambridge, MA 02138

RESPONSE (FLUSHING)
S.M.Cohen, Editor
65-30 Kissena Blvd.
Flushing, NY 11367

REVISTA RIO BRAVO
C.N.Flores, Editor
Box 190
San Ygnaico, TX 78067-0190

RICHMOND AFRO-AMERICAN
R.H.Boon, Editor
301 E.Clay Street
Richmond, VA 23219

ROANOKE TRIBUNE
C.A.Whitworth, Editor
P.O. Box 6021
Roanoke, VA 24017

S A Y N
S.& J. Tretina, Editors
Summit Impressions, Inc.
Highway 36; Airport Plaza
Hazlet, NJ 07730

SCA REPORT Editor
Synagogue Council of America
327 Lexington Ave.
New York, NY 10016

SAN DIEGO VOICE AND
VIEWPOINT
J.Warren, Editor
Box 9
San Diego, CA 92112

SANDARA/LEAGUE
Lithuanian National League
G.J.Lazausakas, Editor
208 W.Natoma St.;Box 221
Addison, IL 60608

SANGER-HILSEN/SINGERS GREETINGS
E.Stone, Editor
3316 Xenwood Avenue
Minneapolis, MN 55416

SCANDINAVIAN-AMERICAN BULLETIN
E.J.Friss, Ed./Pub.
8104 Fifth Avenue
Brooklyn, NY 11209

SONNTAGSPOST
Tribune Intl.Corp.
R.Bell, Editor
10407 Devonshire Circle
Omaha, NE 68114

SONS OF NORWAY VIKING
B.Vanborg, Editor
1455 W.Lake St.
Minneapolis, MN 55405

SOURCE (NEW YORK)
M.I.Glickstein, Editor
City College of New York
Finley 235
133rd.St.& Convent Ave.
New York, NY 10031

SOUTHERN ISRAELITE
V.Golgar, Editor
Box 77388
Atlanta, GA 30357

SOUTHEAST JEWISH CHRONICLE
E.F.Friedman, Editor
314-B.N.Robinson St.
Oklahoma City, OK 73102

SOVIET JEWRY ACTION NEWSLETTER
Student Struggle for Soviet Jewry
c/o J.Birnbaum
210 W.91st Street
New York, NY 10024

STARK JEWISH NEWS
Canton Jewish Comm.Fed.
A.Belb, Editor
2631 Harvard Ave., N.W.
Canton, OH 44709

STEALING OF CALIFORNIA
Native American Training Association Institute
B.Delaney, Editor
Box 1505
Sacramento, CA 9580

STRAZ/GUARD
W.Cytowska, Editor
1002 Pitston Ave.
Scranton, PA 18505

TATRZANSKI ORZEL/ TATRA EAGLE
Polish Tatra Mount Alliance
T.V.Gromada;J.Kedron, Eds.
264 Palsa Ave.
Elmwood Park, NJ 07407

TEVYNE
Lithuanian Alliance of America
G.Meilunas, Editor
307 W. 30th Street
New York, NY 10001

TEXAS JEWISH POST
J.A.Wisch, Editor
Box 742
Fort Worth, TX 76101

TULSA JEWISH REVIEW
D.Aaronson, Editor
2021 E. 71st. Street
Tulsa, OK 74136-5408

TWIN CITY COURIER
M.Kyle, Editor
3637 - 4th Ave. So.
Minneapolis, MN 55409-1324

UFAHAMU Editors
UCLA African Studies Center
405 Hilgard Ave.
Los Angeles, CA 90024

UMOJA Jour.of Black Studies
W.M.King, Editor
Univ. of Colorado; Box 294
Boulder, CO 80309

UPTOWN-Minisink Townhouse
G.Galdney, Editor
646 Lenox Ave.
New York, NY 10037

URBAN LEAGUE REVIEW
W.DeMarcell Smith, Editor
Rutgers University
New Brunswick, NJ 08903

VIENYBE
Jonas Valaitis, Editor
192 Highland Blvd.
Brooklyn, NY 11207

VIEWPOINT
J.Warren, Editor
Box 95
San Diego, CA 92112

VIGIL/HA MISHMAR
R.Newman, Editor
80402 Freyman Dr.
Chevy Chase, MD 20815

WASHINGTON AFRO-AMERICAN
A.M.Carter, Editor
628 Eutaw Street
Baltimore, MD 21203

WASHINGTON LIVING
Spears Pub.Co.; S.Spears,Ed.
6506 McCahill Dr.
Laurel, MD 20707

WIN AWEN NISITOTUNG
206 Greenough Street
Sault Saint Marie, MI 49783

WISCONSIN JEWISH CHRONICLE
L.A.Hankin, Editor
1360 No.Prospect Ave.
Milkwaukee, WI 53202

YIDDISHE KULTURE
I.Goldberg, Editor
Rm.2121; Suite 203
1123 Broadway
New York, NY 10010

YOUNG JUDEAN
M.Newman, Editor
50 W.58th Strteet
New York, NY 10019

YOUNGSTOWN JEWISH TIMES
H.Alter, Ed./Pub.
Box 777
Youngstown, OH 44501

Appendix B

PROJECT COVER LETTER

REPLY TO: Sandra Jones Ireland
R.R.4; Ferry Road
Cornwall, Prince Edward Island
CANADA COA 1HO

Dear Editor/Publisher:

Enclosed is a questionnaire designed to find out about your publication. This questionnaire is sent to you as part of an Independent Study Project I am doing through the English Department at Iowa State University in Ames, Iowa.

PURPOSE OF PROJECT:

This project is a study of ethnic-interest periodicals published in the United States. From this information an annotated bibliography of the ethnic-interest periodicals published in the U.S. will be developed for free-lance writers (academic and general interest) and photographers, as well as a scholarly paper about ethnic-interest publications.

BACKGROUND:

A review of the literature reveals sparse information about the numerous ethnic periodicals published in the U.S., and out of this discovery, this independent study project was developed.

There is NO CHARGE for listing your publication in this

completed project. Because this project was initiated for independent study class credit, it is necessary that the following ISU departments be provided with a copy: English, Journalism, ISU Library, Office of International Students, and at request, Institute of Island Studies, University of Prince Edward Island, Charlottetown, PEI, and project monitors.

Sincerely yours,

Sandra Jones Ireland

cc: file
Zimmerman
Davies

(Author's note: The contents of this letter were changed slightly for the second mailing.)

PROJECT QUESTIONNAIRE

This survey is being conducted as a result of an Independent Study initiated in 1987 through the English Department of Iowa State University, Ames, Iowa, for potential publication in a scholarly journal and reference book by: Sandra Jones Ireland, AA, BA

R.R.4, Ferry Road;
Cornwall, Prince Edward Island CANADA C0A 1H0
Phone: (902) 566-1427 (Atlantic Time)

PROJECT MONITORS:

Zora D. Zimmerman, Ph.D. and Phillips G.Davies,Ph.D.
Iowa State University
Department of English; Ross Hall
Ames, Iowa 50011

Publication Name:______________________________________

Publisher:____

Address:____

____

City State zip code

Telephone: Area Code ( )______________________________

Editor or Editorial Contact:____________________________

Date publication established:___________________________

Circulation: Total:_______ Domestic:______ Intl.:____________

Circulation numbers: Subscription Rate/fee:

Controlled:______ Domestic:____________

Subscription:_______ International:_______

Publication frequency: Daily:_____ Weekly:____ Mo.______

Bimonthly:______ Quarterly:______ Other:___________

Advertising accepted: Yes:____ No:____

If yes, Display ads:____Classified:____ Deadline:___________

Format: Magazine:_____ Newspaper:_____ Tabloid__________

Size:_________

Print Process: B/W only: ________ B/W with color: ______

Over, please

Paper type: Newsprint:_____ Glossy: _____Other:_______________

Paper color: White:_____Buff______Other:__________________

1. How would you describe the ethnic interests of your publication?

2. Do you have non-ethnic-interest readers (institutions,etc.) outside the specific ethnic audience of your subscribers?
Yes:_____No:_____ If yes, please describe:

3. What languages are used in the text of your publication?

4. What percentage of your publication is published in languages other than English?

5. Do you prefer manuscripts in languages other than English?
Yes:_____ No:_____ No preference:_____

6. How do you describe the editorial content (the mixture of news, articles and advertising) of your periodical?

Next page, please

7. Freelance articles accepted? Yes:_____ No:_____
   SASE required: Yes:_____ No:_____
8. If no, staff assignment only? ____ Agent referred?_____
9. Query necessary? Yes:____ No:_____ No preference:______
10. If yes, which is preferred? Telephone:____ Letter:_____
11. If you accept or use freelance ideas, but not articles written by freelance writers, do you pay for the story idea?(kill fee)Yes: _____ No:_____
12. If yes, how is payment calculated?________________

13. Do you pay for freelance articles? Yes:___ No:____ If yes, amount is calculated on: Flat fee:_____Per word:______Per column inch______ News story:______ Feature:______ Other(describe):

14. Freelance photographs accepted? Yes:______ No:______
15. If no, staff assignment only:___ Agent referred:______
16. Photo credits? Yes:_____ No:_____ Payment: Yes:____ No:_____
    If yes, how calculated?

17. What tips do you have for contributors?

RETURN QUESTIONNAIRE TO: Sandra Jones Ireland,AA, BA;
R.R.4; Ferry Road
Cornwall, Prince Edward Island CANADA COA 1H0
Phone: (902) 566-1427 (Atlantic Time)

Selected Bibliography

Harney, Robert F., ed. "The Ethnic Press in Ontario." Polyphony. Spring/Summer. Vol.4, No.1. *The Bulletin of the Multi-Cultural History Society of Ontario*. Toronto. 1982.

Kelly, James, et.al. "In the Land of Free Speech." *Time*. 8 July 1985, p. 95.

Kessler, Lauren. "The Dissident Press." *Alternative Journalism in American History*. Beverly Hills: Sage Publications, Inc., 1984.

Lynch, Audry L. "Don't Overlook the Ethnic Publications." *The Writer*. December 1984, p.25-26.

Miller, Sally M. *History of the Ethnic Press in the United States*. Westport, CT.: Greenwood Press, Inc., 1987.

Murphy, James E. and Sharon M. Murphy. "Let My People Know." *American Indian Journalism (1828-1978)*. Norman: Univ.of Oklahoma Press, 1981.

Murphy, Sharon. "Other Voices." *Black, Chicano and American Indian Press*. Dayton, OH.: Pflaum/Standard, 1974.

Neff, Glenda Tennant, ed., "Ethnic/Minority." *The Writer's Market*. Cincinnati, 1988.

Park, Robert E. "The Immigrant Press and its Control". *Americanization Studies*. Allen J. Burns, Director. New York: Harper & Brothers, Publisher, 1922.

Thornton, Jeannye and Melody Harris. "Why Ethnic Press is Alive and Growing." *U.S. News and World Reports*. 29 October 1984, p. 79.

Ulrich's International Periodicals Directory. "Ethnic Interests." New York: R.R. Bowker/Reed, Publisher, 1987.

Viets, Patricia Powell. Personal communication. History of *Y Drych*.

Wynar, Lubomyr R. "Guide to the American Ethnic Press." *Slavic and East European Newspapers and Periodicals*. Center for the Study of Ethnic Publications. Kent, OH.: Kent State University, 1986.

Index

About the Compiler

SANDRA L. JONES IRELAND is a freelance writer and researcher whose interests include ethnic group issues and ethnic-interest mass communications. Additionally, she is a certified radiologic technologist who has worked and taught in human and veterinary medical radiology facilities, and has presented lectures and published articles relevant to the technology profession.